EERIE WHISPERS

EERIE WHISPERS

Exploring Canada's Reluctant Relationship with Its Ghostly Lore

BRIAN BAKER

Publisher: Meghan Macdonald | Acquiring editor: Kwame Scott Fraser | Editor: Dominic Farrell
Cover designer: Karen Alexiou
Cover image: meunierd/shutterstock.com

Library and Archives Canada Cataloguing in Publication

Title: Eerie whispers : exploring Canada's reluctant relationship with its ghostly lore / Brian Baker.
Names: Baker, Brian (Journalist), author.
Description: Includes bibliographical references and index.
Identifiers: Canadiana (print) 2025023047X | Canadiana (ebook) 20250230518 | ISBN 9781459754744 (softcover) | ISBN 9781459754751 (PDF) | ISBN 9781459754768 (EPUB)
Subjects: LCSH: Ghosts—Canada. | LCSH: Haunted places—Canada. | LCSH: Folklore—Canada.
Classification: LCC BF1472.C3 B35 2025 | DDC 133.10971—dc23

Conseil des arts
du Canada

We acknowledge the support of the Canada Council for the Arts and the Ontario Arts Council for our publishing program. We also acknowledge the financial support of the Government of Ontario, through the Ontario Book Publishing Tax Credit and Ontario Creates, and the Government of Canada.

Printed and bound in Canada.

Dundurn Press
1382 Queen Street East
Toronto, Ontario, Canada M4L 1C9
dundurn.com, @dundurnpress

This book is for those who have an honest interest in Canadian ghost stories and feel at home with the spooky: historians, folklorists, archivists, anthropologists, investigators, mediums, parapsychologists, journalists, and enthusiasts.

It's also for my wife and two kids, who felt my presence haunting a darkened corner of our two-bedroom apartment for the last two years. I love you guys.

Contents

Foreword

Experiences with the paranormal, or what is perceived as the paranormal, do not exist in a vacuum. Unlike the purest form of scientific investigation, where a phenomenon is examined without bias, exploring the paranormal exists within a cultural context. What might be a mischievous spirit to one person is a fairy to another, a djinn to someone else, a trickster to a fourth witness. We filter these fleeting, ethereal encounters through our cultural lenses. Objects moving seemingly on their own, the poltergeist phenomenon, has been attributed to ghosts in some cases and demons in others. It can depend entirely on the background and upbringing of the eyewitness.

How we attempt to understand the things we cannot explain says a lot about who we are. The growing influence of science or the diminishing importance of religion can change how we perceive what goes bump in the night. As Dr. Brian Regal pointed out in his essay "Darwin Killed Off the Werewolf," as the understanding of evolution spread throughout Western society, the notion that humans could just turn into substantially different creatures, then turn back again, fell out of our thinking and therefore our culture. Instead, we leaned into creatures like Bigfoot, "missing links" that fit within early understandings of evolutionary thinking. We now know that there's really no such thing as a missing link, as evolution is a very slow, gradual process. But one thing is clear: Who we are influences how we explain what is unexplainable.

Scholars of strange phenomena sift through a wide variety of cultural material to try to determine why we see what we see. Can all the modern sightings of so-called grey aliens be traced back to one 1964 episode of *The Outer Limits*? Is it just a coincidence that the famous surgeon's photograph of the Loch Ness monster, depicting what looks like a sauropod dinosaur, was taken shortly after the release of *King Kong*, which featured a sauropod rising out of the water and attacking men aboard a raft? It's fascinating to examine the forces at play in our minds when they come up against something entirely novel and potentially terrifying.

If our culture influences how we perceive the paranormal, then how we react to the paranormal must also be considered a manifestation of our cultural identity. How does a country like Canada express its paranormal identity? What does that say about us as a culture?

My maternal great-grandparents, immigrants from the British Isles, were founding members of Toronto's first Spiritualist church. Spiritualism was sweeping through the British Empire, propelled by the momentum of the unimaginable death toll of the First World War. So many, dealing with unprecedented trauma, sought a way to communicate with the millions who were lost. With the innovations in radio communication in the decades prior, was it so hard to believe that communicating with "the other side" might be possible?

Growing up in a household with a backdrop of Spiritualism opened my eyes to Canada's paranormal pedigree. My childhood was one where *Unsolved Mysteries* and *In Search of...* were constantly on our TV, where books about the unexplained occupied my father's bookshelf, where the strange noises in our Victorian farmhouse on Port Union Road, on Toronto's far east edge, were attributed to a ghost. I loved all the usual stuff a boy my age did: baseball and dinosaurs, trading cards and comic books. It just so happened that the Loch Ness monster, the table-knocking of the Fox sisters, Bigfoot, the Roswell incident — the most famous site of a UFO crash — poltergeists, and mediums were part of my vocabulary, part of my daydreams, part of my culture.

Aside from one family vacation to Disney World, we rarely left the country. Summer holidays meant my parents would pack my sister and me into the minivan, drop our dog off with family friends, and head for the 401 on-ramps. It was on one of these road trips, at an antique store in the Maritimes, when I felt suddenly anxious, almost dizzy. It was then I noticed an old wooden cradle. It had survived a house fire, though its tiny occupant had not. According to the proprietor, a lot of people felt what I had when they came close to it. That wouldn't be the last time these vacations brought my family and me in contact with Canada's paranormal culture. There are many old churches, houses, graveyards, or lonely bridges with a ghost or two attached. Many of our lakes are said to have a resident monster. Our country boasts its own Roswells, the most famous being either the Shag Harbour incident[1] or the Falcon Lake incident.[2] Shag Harbour was the site of an alleged UFO crash in 1967; that same year, Steve Michalak reported a close encounter with an extraterrestrial craft at Falcon Lake.

One big takeaway from a childhood that straddled the border of the normal and the paranormal was how little Canada featured in the shows I watched or the books I read. It also struck me as odd how little the paranormal factored into our culture. I assumed that our culture of roadside attractions would mirror that of the United States, just on a smaller scale, but I didn't see their loud-and-proud embrace of the paranormal replicated here. Sure, we have the flying saucer in Moonbeam, Ontario; the dragon-like statue of Cressie in Robert's Arm, Newfoundland; and the statue of Sasquatch outside the Banff Avenue Mall; but they are all blink-and-you'll-miss-them installations. They might appear on brochures, but that's the end of it.

Why are we, as Canadians, characterized by this identity? Is it simply the polite deference that's expected of us? Should our paranormal activity not garner the same response we see in our cousins in the United States or the United Kingdom? What role might geography or demographics play?

Stories of ghosts, lake monsters, strange lights in the sky, or strange sounds in the dark serve as the myths and folk tales of our day. Through them we see ourselves, our values, our fears. The types and nature of encounters change over time because our values change.

Much of my own work has explored our paranormal history through a cultural lens, whether it be my murder mystery, *Crescent Lake*, set in Lake Crescent, Newfoundland, or my work for the Superstitious Times. Why we believe what we believe, and how we choose to express that, has always interested me. It's what makes us, us.

I don't pretend to understand Canada's paranormal cultural identity. Few people have set out to understand and unravel it. Fortunately, Brian Baker, a journalist with a background in anthropology and a long history of covering the paranormal beat, has taken it upon himself to answer the question of Canada's relationship to our paranormal culture. There are few, if anyone, more suited to the task. The book that follows may ask more questions than it answers, as books tackling the paranormal usually do. But it will better help us answer who we are as Canadians in the face of the unknown.

J.J. Dupuis

PROLOGUE
The Birth of an Interest

My interest in the preternatural, supernatural, folkloric, paranormal — whatever word you use to describe the uncanny — began when I was just a youngster living for a brief blip in the province of British Columbia. There, I had a moment that formed the foundation of my interest in the paranormal — one that both literally and figuratively emptied my four-year-old bladder.

My parents took a trip to Vancouver Island, and I was left with friends of the family. I can't remember their home, but I do recollect that they lived on the outskirts of the city, so there was a rural vibe to it. Additionally, I remember that they had cats and dogs.

On this occasion, I awoke from my sleep in the middle of the night. The blue-silver glow of the moonlight filtered through the window, making everything easily visible. I looked to the door at the opposite side of the bedroom and watched it slowly swing open. I thought one of the cats or dogs was coming into the room with me, so I climbed to the end of the bed to see the critter. But nothing was there. I remember pulling myself back up to the head of the bed, and then, in the opposite corner to where I was sleeping, I saw a black mass. When it began to take the form of a person, I hugged my stuffed Dino, which I probably got from Bedrock

City in Chilliwack, and pulled the sheet over my head. Oddly enough, I fell asleep after that.

Some may call that entity a shadow person. Others may call it a full-body apparition. Looking back, I think it could have just been a manifestation of fear and anxiety. Living in British Columbia during the recession of the early 1980s was one of the most stressful times for my parents, especially since they were without a support system.

Many years later, when I spoke with medium Angel Morgan during what was my first interview for this book, I told her about this incident. She told me that I was put to sleep by the entity. "It was there to protect you because a lot was happening in your life," she said in a small parkette along Yonge Street in Toronto. "There were stresses that you didn't realize … that you were going through, and whatever this was, was actually looking over you and protecting you. You register [the stresses] as a child but they don't come out until you're an adult," Morgan continued, saying that I have a balance between this world and the next.

Her insights fascinated me, but I have to admit that they didn't satisfy me. I decided that I wanted to know more.

Perhaps it's my recognition of my own mortality that has really fostered my interest in ghosts. Since my childhood, I have suffered several serious health crises. I was diagnosed with common variable immunodeficiency when I was sixteen. My body's inability to produce antibodies resulted in my contracting an extremely severe case of chickenpox. This led to encephalitis, from which the scarring resulted in my developing epilepsy. As a result, I've dealt with problems relating to my blood. It abated after one big fight with aplastic anemia when I was thirty-one. At the time, though, my system was in such bad shape that I had to be given anti-thymocyte globulin treatment to shock my body back into a functioning state.

So, thoughts of an afterlife have swirled inside my head, even though these days I consider myself an agnostic atheist. It seems to me that we're just such complex creatures it's impossible to believe our consciousness just ends with the vessel's demise.

I am skeptical of a lot of the claims made by some who say they have observed or experienced so-called inexplicable things. And the "proofs" they offer mostly don't convince me of anything. Nevertheless, I am open to theories and captivated by such stories. I stay up late watching YouTube channel shows that focus on the paranormal, like *Nuke's Top 5*, *Slapped Ham*, or *Sir Spooks*. I confess, part of my interest stems from my desire to expose the tricks used to create the footage of ghosts, cryptids (creatures that have yet to be proven to exist), UFOs, and other phenomena — I want to catch the lie, find the smoking gun. There's a satisfaction in that … but there's more.

Our fascination with the paranormal is interesting in and of itself; the stories we create tell us something about ourselves. That interests me. In an introductory parapsychology course I took, Nova Scotian paranormal investigator Elliott Van Dusen said that the field of study is a social science. That makes sense, as most of the evidence we have when it comes to paranormal phenomena is strictly anecdotal. These stories and what they say about us fascinate me.

I am but a humble arts journalist with a penchant for investigating the inexplicable. I've spent fifteen years in the media industry as a reporter, editor, photographer, and columnist. I've covered everything from municipal politics to fashion shows to sports initiatives. Eventually, I decided I wanted to write about something that *really* piqued my interest. In April 2018, I launched the Superstitious Times, a website that is dedicated to reporting on the paranormal in Canada. I write long features and stories about discoveries, reports, and allegedly haunted locations.

From that work was born this book.

Introduction

> Ghosts bridge the past to the present; they speak across the seemingly insurmountable barriers of death and time, connecting us to what we thought was lost.
>
> — COLIN DICKEY, *Ghostland: An American History in Haunted Places*

I stood in the New Age section of a local bookstore and scanned the shelves. I was more than a little disappointed. There are a lot of books on ghosts and other paranormal phenomena, but the bookshelves sat barren. Sure, Colin Wilson's *The Occult* was there, and there was a glut of Tarot decks ranging from animal themes to pop culture flashbacks like *Friends* — insert eye-roll emoji here — but books on the paranormal were lacking. And the same thing is true elsewhere. Books about famous Canadian haunts are as hard to find as smoking-gun evidence of the afterlife, and they shouldn't be.

Stories of hauntings in Canada remain somewhat elusive — not because they don't exist, but because they are often overlooked, forgotten, or dismissed outright. Mark Leslie, who writes horror and urban fantasy and who is the author of six books of ghost stories, has also had to struggle with the lack of respect for genre writing in general.

"It's not literature and I have to say literature with a snobby tone in my voice. Even Margaret Atwood doesn't admit that she writes really amazing dystopian science fiction," he told me in an interview. "The reality is she's actually writing about our world and that's why she says that.

"But there's such a pooh-poohing of Canadian speculative fiction. It's like, is our arts community big enough to support the popular genres?" he asked.

Independent bookstores rarely have horror sections, and Leslie noted that his most recent book launch in Ottawa was at a bookstore that recognized the genre. The bookstore in his current hometown of Waterloo doesn't have a horror section. So his book ends up in the mystery section, along with Stephen King's books.

"When you think about the way we treat speculative creativity in Canada, it's already a second class, but it's more second class in Canada," he said. "I always feel less embarrassed about the genres that I write in the States than I do in Canada. I feel like I have to apologize more in Canada because it's not normal."

Even though there's a large underground river of interest in ghosts and the afterlife, Canadian publishers — there are exceptions, like Dundurn obviously — do not seem very interested in publishing books on the topics. And this lack of interest seems to be the norm in other areas of Canadian cultural life. If you want to find movies, TV shows, or websites about ghosts and the paranormal, you won't have much luck.

Trying to find an allegedly haunted house is even harder. Most of the paranormal investigators I've spoken to have mentioned that commercial enterprises are reluctant to support them. These businesses don't want to risk offending anyone or sounding outrageous by claiming their hotels, restaurants, or courthouses are haunted.

Lesley Mitchell-Clarke is a hypnotherapist who focuses on dealing with experiencers — those who have experienced troubling alien abduction — as well as past-life regressions. Past-life regression is a method of hypnosis that explores memories of past lives or incarnations.

Mitchell-Clarke moved to Canada from New York and admitted in our interview that she experienced culture shock. She said she couldn't get over how Canadians don't say what they mean out of fear of being judged. Her clients experience anxiety about opening up about the paranormal experiences that they have. Even her Contact TV co-host Wes Roberts has been concerned with being exposed as a person who believes in UFOs.

When working with clients and using past-life regression, Mitchell-Clarke admitted, "I have to spend a good chunk of time making these people feel safe." As a hypnotherapist, she faces a lot of skepticism. "There is a lot of scoffing," she admitted.

I wrote a lengthy feature for the Superstitious Times titled, "Is the Paranormal Seen as a Liability in Canada? Investigators Share Their Thoughts," which explores the challenges faced by paranormal researchers across the country. For the article, I spoke to researchers Michelle Desrochers, Jason Hewlett, Morgan Knudsen, and Elliott Van Dusen, of whom you'll read more on these pages. They all observed that while there's an underground river of interest in the paranormal in Canada, businesses aren't at all interested in catering to that interest. Usually, these investigators are forced to try to prove a location is haunted without being given access to the "hot spots" and have to admit, in the words of *Poltergeist* character Tangina Barrons, "this house is clean."

This lack of receptiveness to the paranormal and the lack of cultural presence — pun intended — has made me question who we are as a country. We have such diversity, but when it comes to the biggest question in life, what comes after it, we're as silent as the grave.

Are we quiet because people are too afraid of being seen as weird, or are we quiet because we as a nation haven't established enough culture to talk about the unknown? I've wanted to explore this subject for quite some time and have only been able to give it the lengthy feature treatment on the Superstitious Times.

Is Canada more than just nature, hockey, beer, and Tim Hortons? (Given the new realities of our world and the looming threat of annexation by Donald Trump's America, we are certainly more than that. But for this book, we'll focus on our hang-ups with the afterlife.)

One of the biggest ways we answer our questions about the afterlife is through the arts. Art is an expression of all of our emotions, and the Canadian government made steps to find ourselves artistically and academically through the Royal Commission on National Development in the Arts, Letters and Sciences, also known as the Massey Commission. In 1949, with the Second World War over, Prime Minister Louis St. Laurent decided that the country needed to find its identity, culturally speaking, or at least differentiate itself from the Americans and the colonialist legacy of the United Kingdom.

The report was delivered on June 1, 1951, and it advocated for federal funding to a wide range of cultural activities: radio and television, a film board, a national gallery, museums, a national library, archives, historic sites and monuments, universities, national scholarships, information abroad, and a Canadian arts council.

The Massey Commission's legacy is still being felt today. It resulted in the founding of the National Library of Canada (now called Library and Archives Canada), the creation of the Canada Council for the Arts, and the conservation of Canada's historic places. Government funding helped wordsmiths like Margaret Atwood, Mordecai Richler, and Timothy Findley get published. Canadian content regulations for radio helped our musicians get airplay. In the late 1960s, artists like Gordon Lightfoot, Joni Mitchell, and Neil Young became famous. They paved the way for The Guess Who, Rush, and Bryan Adams.

But still, the infrastructure was not as solid as many would have liked it to be. Our cultural scene has always had inefficiencies, and perhaps that's kept us from sharing our ghost stories beyond the campfires or kitchen parties of the East Coast. Or is it our humble national character that keeps us more grounded than our gregarious neighbours and colonialist motherland? Perhaps it's simply the case that most do not see the paranormal as a means to financial gain, and so Canadians ignore it, despite the interest in dark tourism. That's the other aspect of Canadians. We don't take risks.

Canadian painter A.Y. Jackson once said that fellow artist Lawren Harris believed that a country that ignored the arts left no record of itself worth preserving.[1] It's an interesting quote. It resonates because Canadians don't invest enough in art. But I've been an entertainment reporter, and I care deeply about the arts, so I am truly biased. Regardless, we've had prime ministers openly mock the arts and label artists as a bunch of liberal elitists. Former prime minister Stephen Harper cut $45 million in federal arts and cultural programs and added that ordinary Canadians did not care about the arts.

So where do we stand when it comes to the paranormal? I keep saying there is an underground river of interest in ghosts, cryptids, and UFOs, but it only comes out at socially acceptable events, as I've mentioned earlier and in my work with the Superstitious Times.

Even though we're a young country, colonially speaking, we have plenty of history in our home and native land dating back to the Land of the Great Turtle, where the Anishinaabe oral tradition speaks of a great flood, and the surviving animals helped the Sky Woman to create the North American continent. Indigenous stories of the supernatural can be heard from coast to coast to coast.

On occasion, there has been real recognition of the paranormal in this country. In 2014 and 2015, Canada Post released special stamps commemorating ten of Canada's most enduring ghost stories: the Ghost Bride of the Banff Springs Hotel, the St. Louis Ghost Light in Saskatchewan, Haunted Fort George at Niagara-on-the-Lake, Le Château Frontenac Ghost, the Northumberland Strait Ghost Ship, Bessie Gideon of the Caribou Hotel in the Yukon Territory, the Headless Brakeman of Granville Street in Vancouver, Marie-Josephte Corriveau, the Grey Lady of the Halifax Citadel, and the oxcart of Red River Valley's Lower Fort Garry in Manitoba. And sometimes the media will report on strange goings-on, like in October 2019, when there were newspaper stories about a strange noise recorded by a Sioux Lookout man, Gino Meekis.[2] But the attention was fleeting.

So, the conversations aren't happening out in public. But there have been some bright spots.

My editors during my community newspaper days, Eric McMillan and Dan Hoddinott, would roll their eyes whenever you referred to a living person as a legend, but when it comes to the sharing of ghost stories, John Robert Colombo is one of those names worthy of the label.

Canada's master storyteller John Robert Colombo is full of Canadian knowledge and famous quotes. He has written many books on Canadian folklore. He's also written about the oral traditions of Indigenous Peoples.

Although I wasn't able to sit down with Canada's "master gatherer" for this book, I did get a quick email from him regarding how he got into writing about the paranormal, and I have sat down with him in the past to chat about Canadiana in the kitchen of his North York home.

Colombo has been a prolific writer, not only about Canada's folklore and its tales of the inexplicable but also of its great minds, having published multiple books on quotes, fascinating facts, and poetry. He was born March 24, 1936, in Kitchener, Ontario, when it was an industrial centre in the province. He was fascinated with the stories told about the Pennsylvania Dutch, who introduced their folklore from Germany, which included hex signs on barns, accounts of witches, and strange appearances and disappearances.

"I found hardly anyone else took them at all seriously," he admitted in an email. "The city's officials favoured discussing how hard working the farmers and factory workers were and praising Waterloo County's businesses and factories."

It wasn't until years later that Colombo found that folklorists did take the stories seriously, but to an inquisitive Colombo, the world around him was rooted in economics.

"In later years, I discovered the universality of such tales and stories, and in my travels in foreign countries, I found such tales contributed to the national cultural expression, but not yet in Canada, where we were ashamed of them, much professing or preferring so-called Christian values," he wrote.

So even Colombo noticed some of our reticence as a country, when it came to the paranormal. When he began collecting stories for his first major book in the genre, *Mysterious Canada*, he listed more than ten Canadian ghost stories that were known throughout the English-speaking world.

"During this period around the turn of the twenty-first century, I found younger Canadians began to acquire a knowledge of local traditions of hauntings — the house at the end of the lane, etc.," he wrote, in his email to me. "They boasted of them, and I began, in a series of publications to identify the houses or ruins and the stories that surrounded them."

But the big challenge, naturally, was litigation. One haunted house account in Winnipeg that was printed in the *Winnipeg Free Press* in November 1907 led to a lawsuit, *Manitoba Free Press Co. v. Nagy*.

"Given therefore the three ingredients of the publication of a false statement respecting plaintiff's property, the absence of bona fides in the publication and special damage following as the result I cannot doubt that an action lies," the judgment read. "In the case at bar I think the evidence only admits of one conclusion and that is that the article complained of was false and was published by the defendant recklessly without regard to consequences, and that in this may be found the absence of good faith which imports the malice which is an essential condition of liability."[3]

Colombo was facing criticism in 2000 when residents expressed concern to him that he was publishing descriptions of their residences and their whereabouts.

"Then the jig was up because it was no fun describing but not locating the locus of the activity, so I focused on historical accounts in a series of Quasi Books that simply reprinted the columns of anonymous newspaper accounts of hauntings," he admitted. "All along my interest in them was historical and social and psychological, not as tourist attractions."

What he learned from the experience was that older Canadians have plenty of ghostly experiences and are more open to sharing them at any time of year, while younger Canadians regard such tales as only suitable for Halloween night.

He did leave me with one line to turn over in my head, one that I feel sums up Canada's interactions with the ghostly and unexplained.

"Ghosts are not creatures of the past, but creatures of the present, and presumably of the future as well," Colombo wrote. "Spirits may love the attention, I guess, as do researchers who enjoy retelling their alleged appearances."

Not only did he give me the benefit of his own knowledge and experience, he recommended works that would help me to better understand the world of ghosts and the paranormal. He encouraged me to dive into the parapsychological studies of Dr. A.R. George Owen and R.S. Lambert, key figures in Canada's exploration of the unknown. Owen was editor of the *New Horizons* journal and founder of the Toronto Society for Psychical Research. Lambert was a BBC and CBC employee who wrote about paranormal topics like Gef the Talking Mongoose and shot a 1957 National Film Board documentary, *The Ghost That Talked*, about the events at the Dagg farmhouse in Shawville, Quebec, in 1889.

✦

Since ghosts are creatures of the past, present, and future, this book will look at all three: stories from the past, social and governmental decisions from the past, stories and reports from those involved in investigating ghosts today, and a nod toward the future. And since studies of ghosts and other paranormal entities are considered a part of social science, figments of anecdotal evidence, it is only best to organize this book through another social science: geography. I'll explore the physical boundaries of our vast country: from the west to the north to the central and the east. Then I'll break it down through human geography. As I mentioned, Canada is so incredibly diverse. This isn't a book about Victorian ghost stories influenced by the British or French, but rather a patchwork. I will share the views of English Canadians, French Canadians, Indigenous people in Canada, and other Canadians as well. By looking at the country as a whole and considering all its various parts and people, the goal is to pinpoint just who is open to sharing Canadian ghost stories, and who isn't.

1

A Beginning

Before examining the ways different parts and peoples of Canada look at ghosts, it's a good idea to view Canada as a whole — its history and culture. And to set that up, I'd like to explore how Brits and Americans look at them.

Across the Atlantic Universe

Art historian, lecturer, and author Susan Owens wrote a great book exploring, in detail, the ghost through the lens of British visual art and literature. For those who love social anthropology, visual arts, and ghosts, *The Ghost: A Cultural History* is an essential read, offering information and insights about paranormal phenomena, chiefly of the spectral variety, around the world and what the citizens of different countries and regions believe.

My early July 2024 Zoom call with Susan Owens started with me cooing over her book before explaining what I was doing with my book on ghosts.

To provide the foundation of ghost lore in Canada, I needed British insight into how ghosts are perceived. So much of our paranormal culture is influenced by our British roots, and she offered plenty on British ghosts.

"When I did my book, I needed to keep a lid on it, because there was so much to say about British ghosts," she admitted. "When I was writing my book, and after I'd written it, I was talking to European friends, and I became more and more interested in what other cultures thought about ghosts."

What Owens found was that the French had ghostly folklore, but that it wasn't a big thing. Germans are the same way. The further east she vicariously travelled through her friends' stories, she found the situation changed: Polish and Czech friends were keen on ghosts.

"What's difficult to tell, really, is whether the people I spoke to were expressing their national character … or if it simply reflects their folklore," she said. "The one thing that was agreed on was that the British are just obsessed with ghosts and talk about ghosts the entire time."

Owens grew up with a grandmother who shared stories about being in an old house, playing the piano, and hearing the swish of silk behind her as if someone were dancing even though no one was there. Even Owens's headmaster at her school told ghost stories when Owens was ten or eleven.

"He just told a really matter-of-fact ghost story of how he was cycling into school one day and he saw his father and he said hello. And then he realized, remembered, his father was dead. It was just one of those weird encounters.

"Maybe it wouldn't happen today. I've got a feeling that teachers are probably a bit more careful about what they tell children nowadays," she said. "I definitely grew up with a sense that ghosts were to be talked of and it wasn't just sort of popular culture.

"[It] was just something that was deeply embedded in the [British] culture, these really interesting things that had happened," Owens added. "Ghosts are part of British culture, and they're so much embedded in every historical building in Britain."

Growing up in a medieval house in Suffolk, Owens was often asked if there was a ghost in her house. People are happy to share their ghost stories in England, even the unlikeliest people, such as retired academics.

"I don't think people are particularly embarrassed in Britain, and it's a bit odd because you would imagine that national character, that we might be, but I think it's just that ghosts are so much a part of the culture," Owens said.

There might have been a time in the 1960s and '70s when the National Trust, the government body that takes care of buildings with historic interest and natural beauty, did not include ghostly literature in its guidebooks, according to Owens, but local guides would probably disclose all the spectral happenings in any given building, whether it be Anne Boleyn haunting Blickling in Norfolk, another headless lady at Corfe Castle in Dorset, or even the floating lights of Dunster Castle in Somerset. The National Trust lists all the hottest cold spots (chilly places in buildings whose existence cannot be explained are allegedly evidence of the presence of spirits) on their website.

Owens has noticed a more liberal approach to the paranormal, and it is quite possible that the openness can thank the pop cultural touchstone TV show *Most Haunted*, with Yvette Fielding, for that shift.

"It's quite likely [that the show helped to make ghost stories more popular on TV] because there are lots of other similar programs in Britain too. So I think it's become quite a thing that people love to see," Owens said. "But certainly, there are groups of people one wouldn't talk to about ghosts. You wouldn't go into a gentlemen's club and start chatting about ghosts. You wouldn't be welcome."

After writing *The Ghost*, Owens found that people frequently shared their stories with her — a common experience, I imagine, for Canadian writers like Colombo, Barbara Smith, and Andrew Hind.

"We're proud of them because they demonstrate just how old the culture is," Owens said, adding one such story from the Treasurer's House in York, which underscores England's ancient ties. In 1953 an eighteen-year-old described twenty or more Roman auxiliary soldiers walking through the cellar walls.

Families who have ghosts tied to a location often feel a sense of status, as their family lineage is tied to the landscape.

"There are all sorts of different ramifications about why people are interested, but at the heart of it, it just seems as though we all want to have that experience and it's about connecting with history," she said. "Because I would be totally thrilled to see a ghost if I went to a historic house.

"They give us a free sense of horror, but also of delight at the same time," Owens added. "I think that's why they're very ambiguous figures — that it's not just the emotions that they give. It's not, we're not just afraid of them."

✦

While pop culture does affect the U.K. perspective on ghosts, it doesn't play a major role. The situation in the United States is the opposite. Pop culture plays a major role in the way the paranormal is presented in America, much to the chagrin of parapsychologist Loyd Auerbach, whose columns in *Fate Magazine* were staple reading for me during the 1990s.

"We're really bound up in the United States, and I'm assuming in Canada to some extent, and in the United Kingdom as well, to pop culture," Auerbach noted in a Zoom call I had with him.

Ghost films made in the United States before television dominated the media landscape were mostly dramas, comedies, or romantic comedies.

"They're not at all horror films," Auerbach admitted. "The horror films diverge to monsters or dimensional beings or aliens.

"It's hard to find a horror or suspense show, except for an episode of *The Twilight Zone* or *Thriller*, that wasn't portraying ghosts as human."

The human element was common in films like *Topper* (1937), with Cary Grant and Constance Bennett, and *The Ghost and Mrs. Muir* (1947), with Gene Tierney and Rex Harrison. Television did return to a more humane interpretation of what a ghost is during the early aughts with series like *Medium* (2005–11) and *The Ghost Whisperer* (2005–10), but Auerbach said he finds horror draws more people in.

"When it comes to the general public, most people don't watch these shows, and their belief in ghosts has nothing to do with a national identity or anything else," he said. "There might be some cultural respect in forms of things, and there are more First Nations ghost stories in Canada. They don't often bleed over into another cultural group."

He did call attention to the "pop cultural BS" trope of a haunted location being built on a haunted Indigenous burial ground. Stephen King's *Pet Sematary* (1983) and Jay Anson's *The Amityville Horror* (1977) use the trope, which after exhausting its element of fear and capital gain has more recently been used as a vehicle for white settler guilt.

To a limited extent, Canada has drawn inspiration from American pop culture treatments of ghosts and the paranormal.

A facet of pop culture, one with definite tie-ins to the paranormal world, especially in the United States, is true crime.

There are a handful of true crime stories from north of the border that have gained popular attention. Some have been truly horrifying. In the cases of serial killers Robert Pickton and Clifford Olson, and the missing and murdered Indigenous women and girls on the Highway of Tears, there is no paranormal component. These reprehensible crimes were committed by despicable and evil individuals. The suffering of the victims of these crimes and of those who loved them remains unhealed.

In the past, such stories as Victoria's Fan Tan Alley, Montreal's Mary Gallagher of Griffintown, and la Corriveau of Quebec City have stayed alive through ghost stories.

Ah Heung Chan was found guilty of murder on June 5, 1889. His victim, You Kum, was a prostitute at one of the brothels tucked away in Fan Tan Alley. He was executed on July 16, 1889.[1]

Mary Gallagher, whom I will mention later in this book, met the business end of an axe. She was a prostitute in Montreal's Griffintown and was killed out of jealousy by Michael Flanagan and Susan Kennedy. According to Sheila Hervey in *Canada Ghost to Ghost*, Flanagan was acquitted of the crime. But Kennedy, who was twenty-three, was found guilty. Gallagher's headless spirit allegedly walks the southeast corner of Rue William and Rue Murray on June 27 every seven years. The first sighting was in 1889.

And of course, there is la Corriveau, the story of Marie-Josephte Corriveau, the woman who killed two of her husbands and was executed on Buttes-à-Nepveu, by the Plains of Abraham. After Corriveau's hanging, her body was strung up in a gibbet at the crossroads of Bienville and Lauzon. Her spirit is said to haunt Pointe-Lévy and the Île d'Orléans.

Now, true crime plays a small role in Canadian ghost stories. However, if one drew a Venn diagram of the paranormal, you'd have a trifecta of ghosts, pop culture, and true crime.

This is tantamount to how the paranormal is presented through the American lens. Everything from horror movies, dark tourism, and reality TV shows like *Ghost Adventures*.

The creator of the *Ghost Adventures* phenomenon, Zak Bagans, is a bit of a pariah in paranormal circles that take their research seriously and definitely frown upon the D.C.-born, Illinois-raised TV personality.

Bagans's museum in Las Vegas is littered with artifacts belonging to serial killers such as Ted Bundy and Ed Gein. From what Auerbach shared, however, very few serial killers actually come back from beyond the grave.

The few examples he offered, from the work of his late colleague Carlos S. Alvarado, were those who were wrongly convicted of the crimes and sentenced to death, and returned to right the wrongful conviction.

"It could be that simply their psychology is not such that they may not be interested in sticking around to torment people," Auerbach said.

Regardless of who or what a ghost is, the only way we can communicate or interact with one is through extrasensory perception (ESP). And Auerbach said one aspect of psychical research that has been neglected is whether or not ghosts have ESP.

"If you look at the flip side, how do [ghosts] perceive us? And that has to also be through neurosensory perception," he said. "Years ago, I started teaching a class and giving lectures asking, Do ghosts have ESP? And the answer was yes. If they don't, how the hell are they connecting with the real world?"

The most important idea, Auerbach added, was that ghosts have nothing to do with death. It's what they leave behind when they're alive.

"I liken it to a 1930s movie. If I watch the original *Frankenstein*, there's nobody with that cast and crew that's still alive, but I can still watch it," he explained. "It's a recording, and there's more and more of us that are considering these haunted places that are being visited by so many ghost hunters that they're leaving stuff behind themselves."

That's not to confuse the haunting with a thought form, similar to the Philip Experiment. No, it's more along the lines of stone tape theory, where past trauma or energy is sensed from the stone or the walls of a building. That, of course, brings new meaning to "If these walls could talk."

Stone tape theory does not apply to hauntings, however; it has a bit more to do with ESP.

"The idea of a psychic imprint or residue [what we tend to simply call hauntings] can be applied to repetitive information — perceived emotionally [most common] or in a visual, auditory, olfactory, or even kinesthetic fashion," Auerbach wrote in a follow-up email. "The key is that it is perceived, not sensed [with the physical senses]."

Without getting too esoteric, hauntings are effectively recordings of the emotions, actions, and so on of the living.

"Correlations to unexplained [electromagnetic] fields have been found in many cases and some correlation to the local geomagnetic field," he added. "But it's unclear if those fields are what is responsible for the actual recording and storage of the information or whether they are byproducts of the process in the environment that does this. But there are plenty of cases without any connection to the kinds of minerals/materials the stone tape theory discusses. Still, it's a nice metaphor."

Back to thought forms, also known as tulpas or egregores. They should be more common, Auerbach posited during our Zoom interview, as the intense belief in Jesus Christ and the Devil should bring about entities rather than just pareidolia in toast.

Speaking of the Devil, to those in the parapsychology field, the Smurl case in West Pittston, Pennsylvania, seemed to have the classic happenings of a poltergeist case.

"It stopped after a period, which makes perfect sense because poltergeist events burn out," Auerbach admitted, adding he spoke to two of the reporters that covered the press conference held by Ed and Lorraine Warren, the demonologists brought in by the Smurl family, and they were angry.

"The reporters were mad because [Ed] Warren called the press conference saying that he had video of the demon," he recalled. "One of the reporters asked, 'Can we see the video?' And [Warren's] response was, 'I sent the video off to the Vatican. I can't show it to you.'"

The reporters' anger was just in this instance, as they'd been led to believe there was tangible evidence that the demonic existed. Journalists don't like having their time wasted, and when it happens, they ask the questions that those calling the press conference don't want to be asked.

Naturally, the reporters covering the Smurl family case left.

When looking at the events of a press conference for a haunting through a Canadian lens, one not thoroughly governed by Christian conservatism or satanic panic, it's easy to see how woo-woo the Warrens can appear. Perhaps because of Canada's seemingly secular public sphere, we avoid wading into waters of the demonic lest we sound just a little like we're wearing a sandwich board and ringing a bell down on the main street.

When I asked Auerbach how much damage the Warrens did to the field of parapsychology, he admitted that it was minimal because the Warrens did not tie themselves to the field of study.

"It caused some confusion, especially during the Amityville case because of their claims that they were there with parapsychologists, and Jerry Solfvin, my colleague, was actually the one who was there with them, and he said they were putting on a dog and pony show."

Several clients who had called the Warrens had been traumatized, and Loyd Auerbach followed up with psychologists who were helping families through their ordeals of having their homes declared infested by demonic entities.

"They really didn't do damage to us. They did damage to the general public and propagated that whole demon thing, which Zak Bagans lit on and Ryan Buell and all these shows have taken up the banner."

Now that the Warren estate has been seeing its stories shared on the big screen, the demonic and supernatural horror genres have been given new legs, which in turn leads many to believe that the simple act of a glass moving on its own across a table is the start of something far more sinister.

"We're trying to determine what is paranormal in a case and what is not," he said. "But I still have people insisting it's demonic.... They just simply associate them with the demonic because of these shows, because of the movies; they're always afraid it's going to get worse."

Christian fundamentalism does pose a challenge to investigators like Auerbach, but so does pop culture, where the horror movie scares need to dabble in one-upmanship just to keep the audiences coming to the theatres.

Canada's Pop Culture

Although my conversations with Loyd Auerbach and Susan Owens happened after my talk with *Rue Morgue* journalist Paul Corupe, pop culture was the common thread among the three interviews.

Canada's popular culture, chiefly horror, tends to focus on the man vs. nature theme, as well as the body horror of films like *The Brood* and *Videodrome.*

I was a volunteer photographer for Corupe and his colleague Andrea Subissati during their horror genre series *The Black Museum: Lurid Lectures for the Morbidly Curious.* If you want to know about horror, Subissati and Corupe are two of Toronto's greatest minds. Subissati is the executive editor of *Rue Morgue* magazine, Canada's version of *Fangoria.*

Corupe writes for *Rue Morgue* as well as for a website called Canuxploitation, which has the call to action: "Since 1999, Canuxploitation.com has been exploring and documenting the murky world of Canadian 'exploitation' cinema. With an emphasis on the past, our dedicated review team digs into dusty VHS deletion bins, combs through dollar store DVD racks and braves the wasteland of late-night TV to investigate and reclaim Canada's once-forgotten B-movie tradition with style and humour."

Back to cinema, outside of the American-Canadian co-production of *The Changeling,* the Canadian film industry has avoided the ghost story. *Astraea,* a short film directed by Rouzbeh Heydari, is the only other Canadian production I can think of that channels ghostly lore.

Speaking of lore, our literary scene has used ghosts simply as metaphors. Southern Ontario Gothic was a subgenre that grew from a 1972 interview Timothy Findley had with writer Graeme Gibson. Some of our literary juggernauts included under that tiny umbrella are Margaret Atwood, Robertson Davies, Jane Urquhart, Marian Engel, James Reaney, and Barbara Gowdy.

Atwood's *Alias Grace* really hits the reader on the nose with its references to the supernatural, while the Netflix miniseries watered down the ghostly elements by implying the main character, Grace, was experiencing auditory hallucinations. In the past, TV has embraced the inexplicable through Canadian productions like *Poltergeist: The Legacy, The Outer Limits,* and *PSI Factor.*

I sat with Corupe in the dimly lit Caledonian, a whisky bar on the border of Old Toronto's Little Italy and Trinity Bellwoods neighbourhoods.

"*Changeling* is the one that immediately jumps to mind, but in terms of just straight hauntings, I cannot think of a ton," he said. "It's more legends and more landscape, body horror, gross monsters, and disgusting creatures."

Shadow of the Hawk was the first film that Corupe could think of as supernatural. Jan-Michael Vincent and Chief Dan George star in the supernatural thriller that follows the grandson of a shaman as he returns to the wilderness and encounters malevolent forces. Throughout the evening, more obscure films from Canadian filmmakers crept into Corupe's head, including *Ghostkeeper* and *The Amityville Curse*. The former brushes on the lore of the Wendigo, while the latter is self-explanatory for any horror movie fan. It's about the infamous DeFeo residence in Amityville, Long Island.

In hindsight, I never mentioned the two *Grave Encounters* films, which play on the trope of paranormal investigators in a former asylum.

Still, four supernatural films over five decades raises the question: Why aren't there more Canadian ghost stories shared through the medium of film? The Canadian film industry does not have the output that Hollywood does, and given that lack of production, there is less horror produced.

"Maybe it's just a function of Canada not making a lot of films the last twenty-five years or so," Corupe said. "And even from that, there weren't a lot of horror films.

"You had that boom of horror films in the 1970s and early '80s, and then as the money dried up, everything went to TV," he added. "So you have all these directors doing *Friday the 13th*, *The Outer Limits*, and the last season of *The New Twilight Zone*, which would've had ghost stories."

It's not that Canadian producers don't want to make shows about ghost stories, but the history, in terms of Victorian Gothic, is not there to provide the bedrock for such a culture in Canada.

"Ghosts are England. It's a thirteenth-century abbey. It's M.R. James and he's writing a book about freaks. Even in the United States, you have Victorian houses. There's not a lot of history there," Corupe said. "I don't know that Canada has the history. We do, but it's not preserved in the same way.

"It's not preserved extensively. We don't have these two-hundred-, three-hundred-year-old homes. Some, but definitely not as much as England."

Most of Canada's oldest buildings are located in Quebec or the Maritimes. They're either legacy structures of different religious institutions, remnants of the Hudson's Bay Company's glory days, or military bases.

Fort Anne was originally built in 1629 in Annapolis Royal, Nova Scotia, one of Canada's oldest settlements, and was later rebuilt in 1708. Other houses in Nova Scotia feature the de Gannes-Cosby House and the Adams-Ritchie House. The two former buildings have ghost stories, but the Adams-Ritchie house does not.

In Quebec, the Maison des Jésuites-de-Sillery was built in 1637 and the Moulin á vent de Grondines (a windmill) was built in 1674 and is located along the St. Lawrence River in Grondines. The Maison François-Jacquet-dit-Langevin, which is a five-minute walk from the Château Frontenac in Quebec City, was built in 1675 and is now home to the Restaurant Aux Anciens Canadiens.

Regardless of our limited stock of historical buildings, Corupe freely admits that horror fans are open to talking about the paranormal.

"Horror fans will easily open up about it, even if unprompted. I don't think I've ever asked anyone directly," he said. "They're used to seeing that stuff; maybe not in Canadian horror films, but we watch so many, it's such a common cultural trope that it's easy for them to talk about it."

One of the shows that came up, especially when it comes to ghost stories, was *Creepy Canada*, hosted by Ontario storyteller Terry Boyle, and later Brian O'Dea, who is also known in media circles as a former drug smuggler and as Kevin O'Leary's adviser on the show *Redemption Inc.*

"We're picking up the cues that we've seen in other movies," Corupe said. "We're picking up *Poltergeist* cues, we're picking up *The Haunting*, all those things that set the bar in terms of what a ghost story is, what a ghost story should do, what ghosts look like, how they behave is just based on the common lore."

When it comes to themes that are Canadian-specific creeping into horror, the idea of man vs. nature and the challenges of being taken from one's home or experiencing medical or institutional harm are the main ones. As Canada continues to deal with its dark history with the Canadian Indian residential school system, as well as the Sixties Scoop, one of the key historical influences in horror is institutional or colonial trauma.

But it's not the first time.

The MK-Ultra experiments during the late 1950s, titled Subproject 68, were conducted at the Allan Memorial Institute in Montreal. Dr. Donald

Ewen Cameron experimented on children with LSD, paralytics, sensory isolation, and electroconvulsive therapies to depattern the children.[2] Eventually, the children were also subjected to sexual assault and used as pawns to blackmail more funding from high-ranking officials.

Also in Quebec before the Quiet Revolution, was the issue of the Duplessis Orphans, who were wrongly certified to be mentally ill by the provincial government, all because they were children of affairs. The Catholic Church urged mothers who had children out of wedlock to give them up to the church.

With regards to the residential school system, children were taken from their Indigenous families and were subjected to abuse, all in the name of taking the "Indian out of the child."

These grim moments in Canadian history involving children lend themselves to our cinema and our art as a means of processing severe trauma.

"This idea of taking children, experimenting medically on them and the unmarked graves," Corupe said, "it's a common fear of not taking care of our children, not taking care of the next generation properly and experimenting on people without consent have parallels."

The difference between Canadian films and American films when it comes to the trauma of experimentation, like *One Flew Over the Cuckoo's Nest* or other films where there's abuse or electric shock treatment, is that they become a stronger person, but in Canadian films, they're a shell of a human.

"It's never something to get over, or it's something that if it doesn't kill somebody, it leaves scars. In *Happy Birthday to Me,* [the main character] has a brain operation and twenty years later she kills all her classmates," Corupe added.

Pulling the conversation back to ghosts, and why ghosts don't show up in Canadian cinema, we just don't have the mindset or historical umbilical cords connecting us to our past.

We talked about how Toronto has changed, as a lot of the historic buildings downtown have been demolished in favour of bland, glass-and-concrete condominiums and mixed commercial-residential buildings.

"Toronto always tears down everything," he said. "I was, like, that's not true, and then I was … oh yeah, it's totally true."

Ghosts, when it comes to pop culture, are rarely from the modern era.

"They're these historical ghosts," Corupe said, with a laugh. "They're almost always from another period of time with different beliefs and it's never a ghost from ten or fifteen years ago. It's always a Victorian ghost."

History in Canada, perhaps just in Toronto, is not preserved in the same way that a lot of cities or communities around the globe with a history of ghosts are.

When the Quiet Revolution was happening in Quebec, films being made in Montreal did elicit a fear of going too far and loosening the grip of the Roman Catholic Church. *The Pyx* and *The Possession of Virginia* were the result of a new liberation within Quebec. The demonic came to light, quite possibly at the same time as *The Exorcist*.

The question for Corupe shouldn't be "Do ghosts exist?" because whether or not they do, they have had a massive influence on people. "They've had such a profound influence on so many things that it doesn't matter," he said. "They effectively exist, but if you want to just say the way they help us deal with feelings of guilt or feelings of the past or our relationship with history."

The way Canadians deal with our past may not manifest itself in ghost stories, but it certainly does come out by way of medical experiments, scars from past tragedies, like in *The Sweet Hereafter* (1997), or the natural environment, like in *Black Mountain Side* (2014) or *Blood Quantum* (2019).

But where we lack in film, we certainly make up for in television.

✦

Now, there may not be any modern ghosts in Canadian cinema, but when it comes to television series that share the stories of Canadians, Americans, and Britons, reality TV contributes that element to pop culture.

Since the popularity of *Most Haunted* in the United Kingdom, there's been a glut of paranormal shows from *Ghost Hunters* to *Ghost Adventures* to *Paranormal Lockdown* to *Paranormal State*.

Although Auerbach told me that these shows are excessively in the mainstream, their hosts such as Amy Bruni, Zak Bagans, and Jason Hawes have become niche cultural icons.

Canada has had a few shows in the paranormal investigation vein, like *The Girly Ghosthunters*, *History's Most Haunted*, and *The Other Side*, but their presence within our borders is not to the paranormal convention-spawning extent that our neighbours to the south have.

Still, Canadian production companies are responsible for plenty of ghosts shows like *Haunted Hospitals*, *Paranormal Survivor*, *Paranormal Revenge*, *Maritime Haunting*, and *Hotel Paranormal*.

I worked with Tobin Long during season 4 of *Haunted Hospitals*. It was a relaxed experience, and my first being a subject matter expert on a TV show. So, somewhere in the United States, people are watching me in one of four episodes of *Haunted Hospitals*.

Long was a patient producer, and when I was a newbie, we talked at length about everything from horror movies to baseball to the paranormal.

If anyone has the pulse on what the average Canadian thinks about ghosts, it would be him.

"If you're speaking specifically about Canada, yeah, it's hard to get people to share their stories," he said, during a March 2024 phone conversation. "It's a bit of a stereotype, but Canadians are more reserved than Americans. Americans, for whatever reason, culturally, they don't mind."

Long expanded on his latter point by saying that whenever there's an opportunity to become the centre of focus, especially through the medium of TV, people latch onto it.

"It's sort of that American dream of being discovered," he added.

In the paranormal story zone, people are more vulnerable. They are talking about something that may make them appear to be unhinged.

"There's a hesitation for people to put themselves out there, to make themselves vulnerable to criticism about how they think and feel about an experience that no one has maybe experienced," Long admitted. "Which leads to this double-edged sword that there are people who have these scary experiences that they can't explain, so hearing other people talk about them is a form of catharsis for them."

During the shooting of shows like *Paranormal 911*, *Paranormal Nightshift*, and *Haunted Hospitals*, Long spoke with Britons about their experiences with the uncanny, and he noticed that there was a different vibe to them.

"There seems to be a cultural divide between North America and especially the United Kingdom. From what I can see, from what I've listened to the people's stories and what their experience is, and it's a bit of a stereotype, but they seem to be okay with the idea that spirits are living amongst them," Long told me.

There's an element that is more accepting, more grounded spiritually, rather than anything that could be labelling a spirit as "morally bankrupt."

"People in the U.K. see spirits as just the living energy of people that were once there — their friends and family that continue to visit them and interact with them on some level," he said. "Whereas, in the U.S. it's not just the spirits of the dead, it's the element or the embodiment of something evil that is coming into people's lives."

Even the beliefs of the Indigenous Peoples in North America are different from the Eurocentric, as they are more open to what is just matter-of-fact. What's totally on brand for Canadians is the lack of risk-taking. However, there isn't that element of being evil.

Long worked for four seasons on *Haunted Hospitals* and, as the show progressed, it became easier for people to share their ghost stories that took place in hospitals, hospices, or long-term care facilities.

"We just had a better pipeline connected to certain communities that are more where you are more likely to find those people who have a story to share," he said, adding there were three categories of people that would come forward with stories: patients, visitors, and hospital staff. "It was the hospital staff stories that really make that show work well because those are people that are supposed to be ruled by logic, but logic didn't always dictate what they experienced."

When more nurses started sharing their stories, more doctors opened up to share their experiences. However, a majority of people had either an interest or previous experience. The most interesting stories, and arguably the hardest to find, were those who didn't believe until they had an experience.

Throughout his work on all the paranormal shows, one thing has changed with Long's approach. He no longer listens to be scared, but he listens for the pure experience.

"I definitely have a different feel for what I think is a really viable or very credible paranormal experience," he admitted. "At one level, there are a lot of people who are dealing with some sort of trauma and they've compartmentalized that trauma in some form, so they're projecting an interpretation for themselves of what might have happened.

"Then there are those people that feel very insecure about their spirituality, so they're projecting that insecurity into something that, for them, may be questioning their spirituality," he added. "Something's happened in their lives, so they're having inner conflict in their mind about how the world actually works."

What is a credible paranormal experience to Long is people who were never open to the paranormal and then experienced something they cannot explain and that causes them to second-guess their understanding of the world.

"If anything, it's made me more cynical, but it also has made me more willing to listen to people's stories more with a more open mind," he said. "You want to understand why [they] think it's not A and not B."

Cynicism was a common bond for my family, especially when it came to organized religion. It never factored into our perceptions of the afterlife or ghosts.

Whenever we touched on the ghostly, my mom would tell me, "You don't know what happens until you die." We weren't very religious, so talk of meeting our maker or going to heaven (or hell) was not commonplace — unless, of course, I misbehaved and was catching hell for it.

Whenever that happened, I'd be threatened with some plight that would make Wednesday Addams shudder: Bible camp or Sunday school. Looking back, those were probably empty threats.

Humour aside, ghosts are a common bond throughout the world. Every culture grapples with what comes after our earthly vessels expire.

What better place to start than with a spiritual renaissance that took over the Western world from the 1840s to the 1920s.

2

The Philip Experiment and Spiritualism

Before moving on to our nation's tales of the uncanny, another important part of Canada's ghost culture needs to be looked at: Spiritualism. Followers of the movement, which began in England in the mid-nineteenth century, believed that it was possible to communicate with the spirits of the dead. To do that, séances, led by mediums, were held. People anxious to reconnect with their departed loved ones sat in darkened rooms, holding hands with others, while a medium called on the spirits of the dead, asking them to make contact.

The movement became wildly popular, and people in other countries, including Canada, soon formed Spiritualist "churches." Dan Aykroyd's father, Peter H. Aykroyd, would co-author a book with Angela Narth about Spiritualism in the Western world — *A History of Ghosts: The True Story of Séances, Mediums, Ghosts and Ghostbusters* — covering everything from the advent of the Fox sisters to electronic voice phenomenon. Although the elder Aykroyd did not belong to the Toronto Society for Psychical Research (TSPR), he would write about it in this book, particularly its creation of what has been called "one of the most famous paranormal experiments ever conducted."[1]

Dr. A.R. George Owen; his wife, Iris Owen; and others, including Margaret Sparrow, a former chair of Mensa International, conducted a thought experiment in 1972 where they created a spirit through human will. The group conjured up a character, which they named Philip Aylesford, at séances. The character and his background were wholly fictional.

In *A History of Ghosts*, Peter Aykroyd writes about being present at some of these séances. His experiences helped plant the seeds of one of the biggest pop cultural phenomena of the 1980s: *Ghostbusters*.

The Philip Experiment

I met with Rob Neilly in October of 2023. I'd spoken with him about other paranormal topics, chiefly UFOs, but that night we were chewing the fat over his experiences with the TSPR.

He had always been interested in the paranormal and started correspondence with George Owen when he was sixteen. At that time, he was too young for the TSPR, but once he turned eighteen, he joined the ranks and participated in experiments that explored parapsychological phenomena.

"I was the youngest member for the longest time," he admitted. "I'm surprised they didn't think I was bonkers because I sent them some handwritten material.... I wanted to go find out how real this was and if I had any psychic capabilities. So, they took me in. My God, I was so lucky."

Neilly had already performed séances and other psychic experiments. He joined the society just as they were exploring the depths of a thought form, better known as Philip.

Now, in the 1970s there wasn't as much of a stigma associated with the paranormal. Neilly joked that coming out of the 1960s, thought was freer. Coming out of the sixties, he would hear about the Toronto Society for Psychical Research and the Church of Satan on the AM radio dial.

The Church of Satan was spawned by Anton LaVey and rose to prominence in San Francisco in 1966.

"I'm this fifteen-year-old listening to the radio on a Halloween night, and they said there's this society for paranormal research in Toronto, the Society for Psychical Research." It was the perfect setting for a young man experimenting. He acted as a physical medium.

The group of four were all under the age of sixteen and were family members and friends of the family. They held the séances in his Toronto home and there, inexplicable events would occur.

"I didn't produce anything, but there were tons of special effects, believe it or not," Neilly said. "There were four of us and we all experienced the same thing. So, it wasn't collusion. It wasn't a hallucination. It was like — holy shit! We had a series of them so we stopped."

The experience that jarred him though was when the locked door to the room was unlocked and footsteps crossed the floor right in between the four teens. "It was spectacular," he recalled. "Then a couple of other times we had stuff set up on a table and it seemed to be moving. We all jumped and turned the lights on. I thought mediumship, this is something I'm destined for."

Alas, he admitted he wasn't sure if he had the discipline. However, he learned that the Spiritualist Church of Canada had classes in clairvoyance and psychometry. Clairvoyance is the ability to pick up knowledge outside the five senses while psychometry is the ability to pick up information just by touching an object.

People participating in psychometric reading place their rings and watches into envelopes and pass them up to the platform mediums. The mediums would talk about each object and those in the audience would cry.

All these experiences paved the way for Neilly to join the Toronto Society for Psychical Research. Although Neilly was not one of the eight people who participated in the Philip Experiment of 1973, he knew about it and attended some of the meetings in the beginning. Some of the eight participants were a cross-section of the population: an accountant, an engineer, an industrial designer, a scientific researcher, and a scientific research assistant. Not one of them was a self-professed medium.

They created a fictitious person, Philip Aylesford, complete with a backstory, and conjured him up through a series of séances. Both George Owen and his wife, Iris, wrote about the phenomenon in their books:

> Philip's story in brief is as follows. Philip was an aristocratic Englishman living in the middle 1600s at the time of Oliver Cromwell. He had been a supporter of the king and was a Catholic. He was married to a beautiful but cold and frigid wife, Dorothea, the daughter of a neighboring nobleman. One day when out riding on the boundaries of his estates Philip came across a gypsy encampment and saw there a beautiful dark-eyed raven-haired gypsy girl, Margo, and fell instantly in love with her. He brought her back secretly to live in the gatehouse near the stables of Diddington Manor — his family home. For some time he kept his love nest secret, but eventually Dorothea, realizing he was keeping someone there, found Margo and accused her of witchcraft and stealing her husband. Philip was too scared of losing his reputation and his possessions to protest at the trial of Margo, and she was convicted of witchcraft and burned at the stake. Philip was subsequently stricken with remorse that he had not tried to defend Margo and used to pace the battlements of Diddington in despair. Finally one morning his body was found at the foot of the battlements where he had cast himself in a fit of agony and remorse.
>
> The story continues that Philip has been reincarnated several times since then, but once every century or so his ghost is seen on the battlements at Diddington. The group decided that the present time is a period between incarnations and that his ghost should again be evident. The theory was that if he could be materialized and reassured that Margo had forgiven him and is indeed "on the other side," then he would be at rest.[2]

Initial sessions were held at the home of one of the participants, and they used a simple plastic table with metal legs — similar to those used for playing cards. After three sessions, they moved to another member's home and used a room that was set aside for the experiment.

The floor was carpeted, yet when the raps began in earnest, they were still clearly audible — and they would continue. George Owen would refer to the experiment as a Toronto Breakthrough: Psychokinesis for Ordinary People.

The group even made the film *Philip the Imaginary Ghost* to document the group's work. Now, many were critical of the experiment. John Robert Colombo said this about it in his 1995 book *Ghost Stories of Ontario*: "The Philip Experiment offers proof of nothing, but it does dramatically demonstrate the dynamics of the séance situation — with its physical and mental mediumship and its reputed 'spirit-communication.'"[3]

Many of the Toronto SPR members were also members of the New Horizons Research Foundation, which released journals periodically during the 1970s. It was rumoured that the University of Toronto (U of T) was involved in some capacity in the field of parapsychology. Psychiatrist Joel L. Whitton and mathematician Stephen A. Cook had co-written an article for the *New Horizons* journal. "Can Humans Detect Weak Magnetic Fields?" was a piece featured in the September 1978 issue.

Whitton wrote several articles about biorhythm, psychokinesis, and the study of psi events when subjects are hooked up to an electroencephalogram, much like Rick Moranis in *Ghostbusters*. He also served as a research fellow of neurophysiology and psychiatry at the Clarke Institute of Psychiatry, University of Toronto.

There were more faculty involved with New Horizons. Also among the ranks was professor J. Norman Emerson from U of T's Department of Anthropology. He also served as president of the Canadian Archaeological Association.

So, during the 1970s, there was an interest in all the things parapsychology, even if Canadian universities didn't have dedicated departments. Today, however, the U of T is mum on any involvement of faculty, present or past, in New Horizons.

"Faculty members have academic freedom, which is the freedom to examine, question, teach, and learn, and involves the right to investigate, speculate, and comment without reference to prescribed doctrine," the University of Toronto Media Relations team emailed me. "A faculty member's engagement with an external organization does not generally imply or create an institutional relationship between the University and that organization."

Subsequently, pop culture even grabbed hold of the Philip phenomenon, inspiring two separate horror movies from the experiment. *The Apparition* and *The Quiet Ones* both heavily drew from the experiment, albeit through a horror lens.

Ghostbusters

We know Dan Aykroyd as Ray Stantz from the *Ghostbusters* movies. His upbringing helped him craft the script for the movie with Harold Ramis. In the foreword to his father's book, he writes about Spiritualism, his family, and the idea of conjuring ghosts.

"Were there fakes? Hoaxes? Many, to be sure, and some would say they were all tricks."

Whether or not the levitations, apports, apparitions, and plasmic material moulded into impressions of faces and bodies were real doesn't matter when it comes to shaping our views of the afterlife. It's allowed us to interpret the uncanny, the Fortean, through a different lens.

It's also made for great entertainment.

"Part of *Ghostbusters'* appeal derives from the cold, rational, acceptance-of-the-fantastic-as-routine tone that Bill Murray, Harold Ramis, director Ivan Reitman, and I were able to sustain in the movie," Aykroyd added. "This element originated from my great-grandfather's interest in the subject and from the books he collected."

Which makes Ray Stantz's current vocation in *Ghostbusters: Frozen Empire*, a proprietor of occult books, all the more provocative. Aykroyd has shared quite a few of the experiences of his character in the movie. He has collected books on the supernatural, shared in the beliefs of Spiritualism, and taken part in age-old rites.

"The drapes are drawn, but there is still a faint light in the room. As the guests file into the parlor, they nod significantly to the seated man and take their places, leaving vacant the chairs on either side of the young man. Once the guests are seated, Grandma takes the chair to the young man's left.

Grandpa follows and occupies the last chair, to the young man's right.... They have come from town to talk to the dead."[4]

While Canada may not have produced a lot of really well-known cultural material related to ghosts, the Ackroyd family has certainly helped to put the country on the map.

3

British Columbia

Speaking of maps, it's time to take a look at the different provinces and territories of Canada to get a better sense of ghost culture in the country. As I said earlier, Canada is a very diverse country, and it's hard to talk about it as one thing. The West is different from the East, Quebec is its own thing, and the North is something else entirely. So, to see what the country has to offer in terms of ghost culture, let's take a tour. We'll start on the West Coast.

British Columbia advertises itself as "Super, Natural, BC." Meant to draw attention to the wild beauty of the province, the slogan also does a good job of calling to mind the spiritual character of the place. British Columbia, Canada's rockiest province, is rife with all things uncanny.

People have been living in our westernmost province for over fourteen thousand years. These include the Tagish, Tsimshian, Haida, Tlingit, Kwakwaka'wakw (Kwakiutl) and Nuu-chah-nulth (Nootka) on the islands. The Dakelh (Carrier), Interior Salish and Ktunaxa (Kootenay) peoples live in the interior. I'll discuss these Indigenous groups in a later chapter. All have their own relationships with the spiritual world, relationships that differ significantly from the ghost culture of the settlers who have come to the province in the last few hundred years.

The colony of British Columbia was founded in 1858 during the Fraser River gold rush, a time that produced more than a few lurid tales of human vice. Murder and violent death were not unknown. You might expect that the Maritimes would be home to the greatest number of paranormal encounters, given that death was as abundant as cod once were in the Atlantic waters, but British Columbia is a much more dangerous place — the lumber industry, the mines, and treacherous coastal shores all take many victims. And life could be cut short in the lumber camps, the mining towns, and the cities too. Although it is a young province, British Columbia boasts a good many hauntings.

Many of these have been chronicled by writers with a fascination for the paranormal. Shanon Sinn (*The Haunting of Vancouver Island*) has written about the lore on British Columbia's largest island, and "Ghost Story Guy" Ian Gibbs has explored the tawdry history of Victoria in *Victoria's Most Haunted* and a number of the spooky stories of British Columbia's biggest city in *Vancouver's Most Haunted.*

Gibbs was born in the United Kingdom and made his way with his family first to Calgary and then to British Columbia. His career in all things spooky began when he worked with John Adams on the Ghostly Walks in Victoria. He now calls Prince George home, but Victoria is in his heart. In the introduction to *Victoria's Most Haunted*, he defines what a ghost is: "energy left behind."

I spoke with Gibbs in April 2024 and asked him a few questions about the best-known haunts in the province. He told me that Riverview Hospital in Coquitlam, Vancouver's Gastown, and downtown Victoria are rife with spectral denizens. Stories about these places are also shared in books by other ghost story collectors, Jo-Anne Christensen and Barbara Smith, the latter being the writer who inspired Gibbs.

Riverview Hospital is situated off Lougheed Highway in Coquitlam. It is a popular spot for Hollywood North projects, with *The Butterfly Effect*, *Final Destination 2*, *Jennifer's Body*, *Case 39*, *Shutter Island*, and a personal favourite of mine, *Grave Encounters*. *Deadpool 2* was filmed on the Centre Lawn of the hospital grounds.

During my time working as an entertainment reporter for *Urban Male Magazine* (*UMM*), I interviewed actresses Elise Gatien (*UMM*, Fall 2011) and Jennifer Spence (*UMM*, Fall 2012). Gatien, who can now be seen as a regular in the TV series *Virgin River*, shot episodes of *Supernatural* at Riverview, and she gave a clear indication of the vibe of the place in her comments to me back in 2011. Gatien admitted that she grew up in Kamloops, which is also home to Tranquille-on-the-Lake, another sanatorium with a ghostly past.

> They shot the show at the abandoned Riverview Hospital in Coquitlam, British Columbia — the venue raised the hair on her neck. "I would get stomach aches going there before because the place just freaks me right out," she said. "I can't even explain it to you. You'd be standing there — and we filmed down in the tunnels a lot — and it was terrifying. You can't work at Riverview and not believe in ghosts," she added. "It's just crazy the energy that's in that place."[1]

Spence, who can now be seen on the Canadian series *The Trades* and played a recurring role on *Family Law*, told me back in 2012 that she was jittery because she had heard stories about Riverview.

> "I do remember when I was shooting Alcatraz being in the makeup trailer and Jorge Garcia was talking about how he was scaring himself the night before and couldn't sleep," she said. "That day we were actually shooting at the non-functional wing of a mental hospital here in Vancouver.
>
> "There are all these rumours and stories about [Riverview Hospital] being haunted and stuff, so I guess it got into his psyche a little bit," she said. "That made the trailer erupt into all these ghost stories, 'We've got to shoot in there in an hour and somebody saw a face a couple of weeks ago in one of the windows of the abandoned building.'"[2]

So, what's haunting Riverview? Well, first we have to dig into the history of the institution. Victoria Lunatic Asylum was built in 1872 and closed in

1878, and the Provincial Hospital for the Insane in New Westminster opened in 1878. The provincial government then purchased land in Coquitlam in 1904 to build a new institution. Riverview included a farm with a dairy herd, which, according to Gibbs in *Vancouver's Most Haunted,* produced seven hundred tons of crops and twenty thousand gallons of milk. It also featured a plant nursery, arboretum, and botanical garden. At its peak, Riverview housed close to 4,300 patients. The East Lawn building was set up to house "acute female patients," the Centre Lawn building housed those with serious mental health issues, and the North Lawn housed tuberculosis patients.

The paranormal activity seems to be localized in the underground tunnels that connect the buildings, as well as the East Lawn. Disembodied voices, footsteps, and breathing can be heard. Security guards have reported seeing apparitions of people in their pyjamas.

In Vancouver's historic Gastown, there is a different kind of ghostly vibe. Identified best by its cobblestone streets and ornate steam clock, the neighbourhood is named after John "Gassy Jack" Deighton, who had a pub in the area back in 1867.

Destroyed by fire in 1886, Gastown rose from the ashes and became the hub for many merchants. During the 1930s, it became the party centre for the city, but after that, it fell on hard times, becoming a priority neighbourhood for the city council. With a new highway proposed in the 1960s, residents protested Gastown's destruction. Fortunately, the neighbourhood was saved, and it is now a trendy place, filled with restaurants, bars, and fashionable shops that attract tourists and locals.

Gastown is rife with hauntings, and Waterfront Station, originally built in 1914, is home to a lot of the stories. One has forever been immortalized on a Canada Post stamp.

The subject of the stamp is a headless brakeman carrying a lamp. The story goes that Hub Clark met his Waterloo while inspecting the tracks around the foot of Granville Street one wet night. He slipped and hit his head on the tracks, knocking himself out. Unfortunately, a passenger train rolled along the tracks and severed his head from his body.

Workers at Waterfront Station and even Ghostly Vancouver Tour guides have witnessed a man in overalls carrying a lantern.[3] One can assume he's looking for his head, but perhaps he's just retracing his steps as an echo of that fateful night's events.

The Headless Brakeman is not the only apparition skulking in the corridors of one of Vancouver's busiest transit hubs. Motion sensors going off once the station shuts its doors give security guards headaches, according to Gibbs, and one women's bathroom has one resident spirit who seems to favour a particular stall. A 1920s flapper has also been spotted in the west corridor dancing away into nothingness. Witnesses who claim to have seen these entities all say they heard footsteps that clued them in to the presence of the spectres.

Gibbs mentions other ethereal presences in his book, such as the apparition that paces the upstairs of the Irish Heather and Shebeen on East Georgia Street. Kimprints on Powell Street and the Alibi Room on Alexander Street are also home to Gastown ghouls. The building that Kimprints is in has been known to have a shadow that the living must contend with, high electromagnetic field readings according to the findings of investigators from the Vancouver-based paranormal investigation group Cornerstone Supernatural, and the barks of phantom dogs in the basement. The Alibi Room, which has been used as a set for movies, has disembodied footsteps, shadow figures in the women's washroom, and a dark, intimidating presence in the basement kitchen area.

Trounce Alley, also known colloquially as Blood Alley, is also rife with stories. One of the more famous features a woman in black who walks along where Gaolers Mews once was, making her way to the steel gate of Blood Alley. At one point, a jail and gallows stood there, so it is suspected she was the widow of one of those hanged.[4]

As mentioned, Victoria is home to a good many hauntings. I've always loved the lore around Victoria's Empress Hotel. One of the four ghosts that inhabit the Empress is a chambermaid, Lizzie McGrath, who fell to her death. With the hotel under construction in 1909, all of the drainpipes and fire escapes had been removed. It is alleged that one night when she was getting ready for bed, Lizzie went to climb onto the fire escape to do her rosary. Being Catholic, it was something she did every night. Unfortunately, she slipped and fell six floors to her death. Her spirit is often seen by the front entrance.

The Fairmont Empress Hotel is said to be haunted by multiple spirits, including an Irish chambermaid named Lizzie McGrath, who plunged to her death when renovators removed the fire escape stairs to her room. The other ghosts that wander the halls are an elderly woman and an adulterous architect.

The architect of the building, Francis Rattenbury, has been seen in the basement of the hotel, near his portrait. He was certainly a piece of work. He spied on a much younger woman and, infatuated with her, demanded that his wife, Florrie, give him a divorce. She would not, and to spite her, he cut her off from all social engagements and cut the power to their home.

Eventually, Florrie gave him a divorce to protect her two children. Rattenbury, realizing he had alienated himself within the Victoria elite, took his new love, Alma, with him back to England. Eventually, she grew tired of him and conspired with the chauffeur, George, to kill him. George was sentenced to death, but Alma was acquitted. With her new love behind bars, she stabbed herself six times in a fit of despair and fell into a river. George survived, however. His lawyers appealed his sentence and eventually, he was released. He was sent to fight in the Second World War. He survived and returned to England to have a family. It seems that Rattenbury's spirit did not find peace in England, and it returned to Victoria to haunt the famous hotel he had designed.

The other two spirits are the usual hotel fare: an elderly woman who has been seen in the tower that was added in 1929 as well as in the gold suites on the sixth floor, and a porter named Bill who continues to work long after his shift is done. Oftentimes, those witnessing the entities in the hotel question their sanity.

Ghost Island

There is no shortage of short ghost stories in Canada, according to Gibbs. He has worked hard to celebrate some of them in the books he's written, but it has been hard work. Getting people to share their stories of ghost sightings isn't easy, he says.

During his work on his books, he always makes it a point to make his interviewees feel comfortable, assuring them that he's not judging them and that he's always on their side. "In Canada, we're reticent to take a stand. We're reticent to say, 'This is what I believe,' because we don't want to upset anybody," Gibbs said. "Americans have no such inhibitions.... We are not like that. We're a lot more cautious.

"On some level, we all fear ridicule," he said. "I understand that. So, if I can head that off at the pass, I'm able to get stuff out of people maybe they wouldn't normally talk about."

Sure, people are worried about being ridiculed if they open up about their experiences, but they can be persuaded. Gibbs has been at dinner parties, and once people have had too much wine, and the topic of the uncanny comes up, that's when people start talking.

He understands that reticence because he has felt it himself. One month before *Victoria's Most Haunted* came out, he realized that by publishing it he was admitting to being interested in ghosts. "I remember thinking very clearly, *Well, this is it. I'm outing myself as a ghost person, and there's no coming back from that*," he said, with a laugh. "I love Barbara Smith's and John Robert Colombo's books, but they're much more reporter style. They describe things, they don't commit."

He does commit in his books, expressing how he was feeling.

"Uh, fuck it," he said, with another laugh. "If I can't bring anything of myself, why bother. I'm not going to be able to write a book that's filled with 'allegedly,' or 'this person claims.' That's just not who I am."

Bringing himself into his books is important for him because he himself has experienced strange occurrences. "I don't go looking for them, though," he said. "I don't want anything following me home." Sometimes, when he visits a house, he'll get a prickly feeling, what he calls a "spidey sense." Whenever he wants to gauge what's happening beyond the five senses, he'll drop his guard. Again, he stresses it's not something he explores. He doesn't look for proof on ghost investigations.

When he drops his guard, he gets pictures. As an example, he recounted a visit he made to a friend's future home. They were explaining that they were going to turn an attic room into a dressing room. Gibbs said an image of a very angry woman in stained clothes in the corner of the room came to him. When he asked what was in the room before, his friend said it was the original owner's wife's art studio.

"Someone takes a bunch of memories and shoves it in the back of my head," he said. "I don't know how to explain it."

Gibbs has often been asked by his American friends how the perception of ghosts in Canada differs from that in the United States. And naturally, the biggest influence is pop culture.

"What did the movie *Ghostbusters* do to ghosts and popular culture?" Gibbs asked. "I love the movie, don't get me wrong, but it basically turned ghosts into just another movie monster — not real."

The movie also implied that any academic institution that funded parapsychology was silly and undermined it.

"People can't get enough," Gibbs told me, with a laugh. "The yelling at ghosts? Oh my God, do you want to drive me crazy? Start being disrespectful to anybody, especially someone who can't fight back."

Gibbs acknowledged that there is one big difference between Americans and Canadians when it comes to ghosts. Our neighbours to the south are very open about their encounters with the ethereal. "Most Canadians, if you say, 'Hey, I'm really looking to hear your ghost stories,' will say, 'I don't believe in ghosts, but ...'" Gibbs said, with a laugh. With a little encouragement, he's found that he can usually persuade the person to share stories they've heard; sometimes they will even share an experience they've had. Still, it appears that Canadians need the comfort to not commit to believing in what they've experienced. Canadians don't like to take risks.

That may be true, but it seems that lack of willingness is stronger in some places than in others. For example, the differences between British Columbia and Alberta are palpable.

"Any area with a coastline seems to have more ghost stories," Gibbs said. "I don't know if it's got to do with the theories around water and energy, but people in British Columbia, in some ways, are more open to it. In Alberta, it's a lot more rigid."

The Interior

British Columbia's coastal communities have plenty of tales of shipwrecks, tragedy, and hardship, but the interior of the province has its share of paranormal offerings too.

Jason Hewlett and Pete Renn are co-founders of the Canadian Paranormal Society and both of them call Kamloops, British Columbia, home. In the past, I've spoken with Hewlett about the undercurrent of interest in the paranormal. He agrees with Gibbs that Canadians are interested in hauntings or alleged ghosts, but they prefer to keep quiet about their interest and will only bring it up when it's socially acceptable to do so. Even then, they aren't likely to take seriously the idea that ghosts are real and that it may be possible to prove it. He and others in the Canadian Paranormal Society do try to do that.

I met with them in July 2023 through Zoom, and the world of the paranormal materialized in our conversation.

"What we find a lot of times is that the so-called stories that go with certain places don't really marry up," Renn said. When they try to document hauntings for TV shows like *We Want to Believe* on Paraflixx, they're trying to grasp the tangible.

"The problem with that is we are in a field where we don't know what we're measuring," Renn admitted, adding that the definition of what a ghost is has not been clearly mapped out by science.

One of the difficulties that Hewlett and Renn face is the abundance of paranormal investigation groups in cities across the province. It's become popular fare, which has created a hindrance to their own investigations.

"The majority of British Columbians are snobs, to put it bluntly," Renn said. "I've tried to approach places, even when I was running the Vancouver Paranormal [Society] site, and [I usually got the same response]: 'I don't want any paranormal group to come in here.' As soon as you mention that word, paranormal, the doors automatically shut."

Hewlett jumped in, stating that although more people are actively pursuing paranormal investigation, there aren't as many people approaching it with the same level of professionalism seen by traditional parapsychologists.

"They're out there for the thrill, and it brings a bad taste to certain things," Hewlett said. "They might get into a place but it turns that place off because of the way they act and portray those locations."

On the other hand, Benjamin Radford, the deputy editor of *Skeptical Inquirer*, believes that the glut of paranormal research groups has a good side as it represents a democratization of the field.[5]

Renn is not so accepting. He feels that some investigators have sullied things, thus creating a disdain for the paranormal research field as a whole. Events were organized to bring tourists in to help keep the heritage sites alive, but proper respect wasn't paid to the places or the people in the stories. And there has been too much attention paid to a few well-known locations. Because of the glut of investigators, doors have become closed to researchers in both his native England and in British Columbia. However, there is more acceptance, Renn says, in England. "There's probably more acceptance there because there's more history there," he said. "Everyone puts that parallel between the history and the paranormal. They're intrigued to know a little bit more."

Hewlett and Renn have also gone on investigations in the United States, in locations like Coeur d'Alene and Gooding, Idaho, and they feel that there is a noticeable difference between Canada and the United States when it comes to acceptance.

"The whole town opened up [when there was] a paranormal group coming to town," Renn said. "When we went to Coeur d'Alene and Gooding, we did historical research, and when we announced ourselves as paranormal investigators, everyone was like, 'Yay!' We were like celebrities."

"The Gooding Inn even rents itself out for paranormal investigations," Hewlett added. "Whereas here, good luck trying to get into half the places. We have to beg, borrow, and steal our way in half of the time."

The challenge for the Canadian Paranormal Society is getting their foot in the door. There are exceptions, though. Hewlett said the O'Keefe Ranch and Vernon Towne Theatre, both in Vernon, are typically open to investigations. Hewlett and Renn have partnered with the O'Keefe Ranch to offer paranormal investigations to the public.

The Sagebrush Theatre, in Kamloops, allowed the team to investigate there for a fee. They had to pay for a member of the staff to be present. Now, that's understandable, but still one would wonder what Albert Mallot would think, having to be chaperoned and all. Mallot was the first man to be hanged in Kamloops, and it is his spirit that is suspected to be haunting the Sagebrush Theatre.

Another concern, both Hewlett and Renn expressed, is that not enough pre-investigation research is done. The advent of TikTok has created a unique challenge for investigators.

"I think it has a lot [of impact]. It has a lot in the worst possible way because all these people are thrill-seekers just running around saying that they're having these paranormal encounters — but they want you to watch," Hewlett said. "How do you know they're not staging stuff? They're using very questionable equipment and saying they're finding stuff."

One piece of equipment that Hewlett found dubious was something called Spirit Chat, which is similar to an ovalus. For those who don't know what an ovalus is, it's a device designed to respond to variations in the electromagnetic field using words from a pre-programmed dictionary.

Hewlett joked that the model he was using was made in the United Kingdom so the unit was showing words like Tudor and wench. "It was fun to watch, but geez, people are looking at this on TikTok and saying, 'This spirit's talking to me and it called me a wench,'" Hewlett said with a laugh.

"What's generally lacking in the field is people having an understanding of what they're trying to measure," Renn added. "We're never getting an understanding of what we're trying to measure [and] the only time we will know is when we're on the side of that realm."

The field is not going to evolve if those who deem themselves researchers don't research anything. Being able to use K-II EMF (electromagnetic field) meters is one thing, but Hewlett and Renn would like to see more investigators who are able to analyze the data properly. If more investigators acted in a professional manner, it would make it easier for them to go to allegedly haunted locations where they're not going to be shunned.

"We should be focused on data collection and repeating experiments and trying to get into the same location multiple times to repeat, come up with theories, and put them to the test," Hewlett said. "You have to get into a place multiple times [to get meaningful results], but many of the people visiting sites just want to get that thrill."

Once some investigators get that electronic voice phenomena (EVP) recording, Hewlett added, they're off to somewhere else. In his mind, they're not taking a very serious, measured approach to the field of paranormal study.

The Canadian Paranormal Society has visited Barkerville, a gold-mining town in British Columbia's interior, and captured an EVP of a historical actor who performed as Justice Begbie. The gentleman who had passed was Tim Sutherland; the EVP recorded a simple but eerie "Go away."

It wasn't an intelligent response to a question, but when staff member Michelle Lieffertz heard it and recognized the voice, Hewlett realized that they had struck gold.

"We captured her actually hearing it. [You could see her experiencing that] in her face; that's the gold that you get doing this job," Hewlett admitted.

Evidence of the afterlife aside, researching the history of sites in British Columbia has presented its own challenges for investigators like Hewlett and Renn.

"When I was a paranormal investigator back in the United Kingdom, I'd go to the local library and I'd be able to research the land and go back to the sixteenth century," Renn recalled. "But B.C., there's nothing. There are ways of finding it, but everyone just Googles it."

The two suspect not much will change, culturally speaking, in British Columbia or within the scientific community because investigating ghosts

While investigating the Barkerville Hotel in British Columbia's interior, the Canadian Paranormal Society's Pete Renn captured the image of a man's elbow poking out of one of the upstairs rooms with his motion-detector cameras.

and hauntings is a "moving target." Plus, thrill seekers may create an environment of punchlines.

"It'll be like *Ghost Adventures* or what you're seeing on TikTok," Hewlett said. "People will just dismiss it because it's just another little bit of sensationalism.

And then there's the issue of money. Canadian businesses tend not to want to do anything unless there is money. To pay them, the investigators must get involved in fundraising.

The former sanatorium in Kamloops, Tranquille on the Lake, won't allow anyone on the property to investigate the paranormal, Hewlett stated. "When I spoke with property co-owner Russell Cundari, a lawyer and member of the original four-party consortium that purchased the grounds from A&A Foods in 2000, he said he had never experienced anything paranormal."[6]

Renn has found that the culture of British Columbia, in general, is flaky and insular. "You're a very fickle bunch, you Canadians," Renn said with a laugh.

Despite these obstacles, British Columbia remains rich with spectral lore. From historic towns like Barkerville, a revenant of B.C.'s gold-mining past, to the silent corridors of abandoned institutions like Riverview, the province offers no shortage of haunts waiting to be explored. Whether dismissed as folklore or examined with a more scientific lens, the province's mysteries endure — whispering to those willing to listen.

4

Alberta

The roots of Alberta's folklore and ghostly stories can be tied directly to Indigenous beliefs, such as the folklore that tells of the Sasquatch and Wendigo. The legends surrounding the hoodoos outside of Drumheller are another example. The story goes that anyone who walks around the hoodoos at night would be struck with an arrow from the "night people." Indigenous people would leave gifts as an olive branch to these entities.[1] Inevitably, some of those stories found their way into interpretations by the settlers. With the introduction of the railway, the first wave of immigration to Alberta from 1867 to 1914, and with the relocation of many Ontarians, ghost stories began to evolve and take on a Victorian flavour.

Still, according to Morgan Knudsen, an Alberta paranormal researcher, the old lore of the province is alive and very active. "[Quite a few of our stories] really tie in with … old lore that's here. You get a lot of stories about … the spiritual side.… [Of course, the fact that those stories are Indigenous] is part of the reason why [they're] not discussed a lot."

The spiritual lore of the Indigenous Peoples in Alberta can also be found in modern paranormal stories, in particular, the stories around the Frog Lake vision.

On April 2, 1885, a group of Cree warriors led by Wandering Spirit attacked the settlement of Frog Lake, killing nine people, including government officials, settlers, and a Catholic priest, Father Léon-Adélard Fafard. The attack was part of rising tensions between the Cree and the Canadian government over broken treaty promises, dwindling food supplies, and harsh policies imposed on Indigenous communities. The massacre was one of the earliest violent incidents of the North-West Rebellion, a broader Indigenous and Métis resistance against Canadian authorities.

Author John Robert Colombo documented the massacre in *Ghost Stories of Canada*, detailing how the Cree warriors also kidnapped two women, Theresa Delaney and Theresa Gowanlock, who were held captive for eight weeks. The attack was not sanctioned by all Cree leaders. Prior to the massacre, Cree chiefs had gathered near Onion Lake, where Chief Big Bear, a proponent of diplomacy, urged against rebellion. He had reluctantly signed Treaty 6 in 1882, hoping it would protect his people. However, a faction of his band, frustrated by government neglect, chose to take action.

A mysterious elderly woman with unkempt black hair is said to have warned the warriors against violence. Later, as government forces pursued the Cree, she continued to caution them.

"No brave can move fast enough to outrun the soldiers who have a thousand bullets for every Indian brave," she told the Cree leaders gathered at a reserve near Onion Lake.

According to some accounts, Big Bear himself ordered her death, and her body was left for the wolves as the group pressed on with their captives.

During their captivity, Theresa Gowanlock later recounted witnessing a strange event: As the Cree warriors watched, the clouds parted over Frog Lake, and the church burst into flames. She claimed the fire was blessed by a pale rider on a white horse.

The vision would be interpreted in different ways. One is that it was a supernatural omen or a sign of impending tragedy. Others speculate that it was a hallucination brought on by the trauma experienced at Frog Lake. Still, the vision itself was not mentioned directly by Gowanlock in her book, *Two Months in the Camp of Big Bear*.

The North-West Rebellion lasted several months but was ultimately crushed by Canadian forces. Big Bear, who had not participated in the violence, was later captured at Frenchman's Butte, along with a handful of other Cree members, on June 26, 1885. He was sentenced to three years in Stony Mountain penitentiary for treason-felony, despite his attempts to prevent bloodshed. Wandering Spirit and six other warriors were later tried and executed for their role in the massacre. The events at Frog Lake remain one of the most tragic episodes of the rebellion, marking a turning point in Canada's handling of Indigenous resistance.

On August 6, 1879, a darker tale emerged. Swift Runner was convicted of the murder of his wife and five children. He also cooked and ate their flesh. It is suspected that he suffered from an Algonquian-specific psychiatric disorder called Wendigo psychosis. Eventually, on December 20, 1879, Swift Runner was hanged at Fort Saskatchewan, thirty-five kilometres northeast of Edmonton.

"Swift Runner was the first legal hanging in Alberta, and up around through Slave Lake, again all these stories of Wendigo and Skinwalkers (shapeshifters of Navajo legend) is really steeped here," Knudsen said. "We were the one-horse town for a really long time. Our haunting stories came later when once buildings started to go up and people started to move in."

"A lot of the legends and lore that you get out of Alberta are pretty creepy," Knudsen said, adding the story of Swift Runner is one that keeps the Wendigo, a malevolent spirit that allegedly possesses humans, alive.

Now, the Wendigo is an entity that has been misinterpreted through a colonialist lens. When I have asked Indigenous sources in the past, a lot are hesitant to open up. When I emailed with Indigenous spirit investigator Erin Goodpipe, who you'll meet later in the book, she was mum.

> I dare not even say the name of this being. There's a little bit of humour in saying that but also seriousness, since in our territory, we have special cultural ethics and protocols in how to care for the speaking of this being (at least with certain Nations and communities) because speaking of it also conjures it to a degree.

Investigators (from left) Michael Browne, Morgan Knudsen, and Jason Hewlett visited the original location of where Swift Runner was hanged in December 1879: Fort Saskatchewan, Alberta.

> Of course, there are different views of this being across territories and yes, this being is that of insatiable hunger/greed so much so (that) the person that has conjured this being, potentially in themselves, lose themselves through it.

However, when the story of Swift Runner (Kay-say-kwyo-chin) is brought into the picture, modern psychiatry crawls into action. Long before pop culture skewed the perception of Wendigo with films like *Ravenous*, *Wendigo*, and *Antlers*, and video games like *Until Dawn* (2015), even before Algernon Blackwood's tale *The Wendigo* (1910), there was the story of a Cree hunter.

A friend of mine from university, Michael D. White, who belongs to the Bear Clan of the Anishinaabeg, once explained to me that the Wendigo is a mindset. I included it in a column about the lack of diversity in paranormal TV.[2]

> "The problem with these stories is the heavily Christian and Western lens," he wrote. "Horror movies and non-Indigenous views have created something out of this being that doesn't represent our own beliefs about what it is and why it exists."
>
> For him, the Wendigo represents what happens when we give in to our self-interest and forget our role to those around us and to other people.
>
> "We become consumed by our individual wants, needs and begin to consume others around us," he wrote.

I'm going to cover the spiritual stories of the Indigenous Peoples in Canada later in the book, but I'd like to explore some of the other Alberta tales of hauntings first.

✦

Barbara Smith is one of the best-known chroniclers of the paranormal in Alberta. She has written a number of books, such as *Ghost Stories of Alberta* and *Great Canadian Ghost Stories*. The first story she recounts in the former is that of the Fairmont Banff Springs Hotel. But she doesn't start with the dancing bride, seen now and then in the Rob Roy dining room performing a solitary waltz (more on her later). No, Smith starts with something more recent.

Most Canadian ghost stories involve a revenant of the long-dead past, but the ghost of Sam McCauley, a former porter at the Banff Springs Hotel, is a more recent addition to the province's ghostly folklore. Reports of his presence began in the late 1970s, with guests and staff claiming he continues to assist those staying at the hotel.

McCauley was a long-time employee of the Banff Springs Hotel, known for his kindness and dedication to his work. He passed away in the mid-1970s, and it was after his death that the stories of his ghostly deeds began to circulate. Some say that because of his deep connection to the hotel, his spirit lingers, continuing to provide service even in the afterlife.

Guests and staff have reported encountering a friendly, elderly porter matching McCauley's description, often appearing when help is needed. Some claim he assists with luggage, only to vanish when they try to tip him. Others have seen him in his trademark uniform, walking the halls before disappearing around a corner. Despite these eerie encounters, McCauley's ghost is considered benevolent, acting more like a helpful presence than a typical restless spirit. McCauley is buried in the Mountain View Cemetery, just thirteen minutes north of the hotel.

Barbara Smith, author of *Ghost Stories of Alberta*, has written about McCauley in her books. However, when she first investigated the Banff Springs Hotel, the management was dismissive of any ghostly claims. "When I first started investigating the Banff Springs, I had heard about Sam McCauley, the porter," she recalled during a March 2024 Zoom call. "[However, the management of the] Banff Springs Hotel told me they were not haunted; they wanted nothing to do with any such nonsense and pretty much told me, 'Don't phone back — we're finished with our conversation.'"

Despite the hotel's reluctance to embrace its ghostly reputation, stories of Sam McCauley's spectral presence continue, making him one of Canada's most famous ghosts.

She didn't give the rebuff a lot of thought at the time. It was something that paranormal investigators have to get used to. She got a great surprise, though, when she started looking into hauntings of Jasper Park Lodge. The difference between how the Banff Springs Hotel and the Jasper Park Lodge reacted was like night and day.

"They said, 'Oh yeah, yeah, are we ever haunted! One particular cabin is really wild,' and they kept going on and on," she recalled, adding that they faxed her all the details.[3]

The building in question is the Point Cabin, where a chambermaid in the 1940s or '50s had been surprised by a guest and fell to her death.

"[Banff told me], 'No way, go away, lady,' [and Jasper gave me] the highest check available; [they told me], 'We're going to get these stories to you.' I thought that was very interesting."

Banff Springs Hotel wasn't the only place to throw shade on Smith's investigations. The Hotel Macdonald in Edmonton also proved elusive when

Barbara Smith attempted to investigate its paranormal activity. Management was reluctant to acknowledge the ghostly legends surrounding the 100 Street NW landmark.

Among the reported apparitions is a man wearing a bowler hat, seen entering the elevator before vanishing without a trace. However, the most famous and unsettling spirit is that of a spectral horse, whose galloping hooves can be heard echoing through the halls of the eighth floor. Some witnesses claim the phantom horse is a remnant of the hotel's early days, when it catered to wealthy guests who traveled by carriage. Others believe it is tied to a long-forgotten tragedy, though no historical records confirm its origins. "They too told me to get lost and never come back," Smith said, adding that the PR person was quite abrupt, interrupting her to tell her that they were done talking with her.

Another Alberta haunt that Smith enjoys talking about is the Deane House in Calgary, one of the city's most well-known paranormal hotspots. Originally built in 1906, it served as the official residence of Richard Deane,

The Banff Springs Hotel is home to several spirits, but the two most well-known stories involve the waltzing bride of the Rob Roy dining room and porter Sam McCauley, who helps travel-weary guests find their rooms.

a superintendent of the Royal North-West Mounted Police. The house was originally located near Fort Calgary but was moved across the Elbow River to its current location on 9th Avenue SE in 1929.

Its adventure across the river, courtesy of its owner C.L. Jacques, made the news in an issue of *Popular Mechanics*. That wasn't its first move, either. In 1914, it was moved from its first parcel of land to the southeast corner of Fort Calgary after the Grand Trunk Railway purchased the fort's site.

Over the years, the Deane House has had a dark history. Richard Deane's wife, Martha, never had the opportunity to reside in it, as she died before moving in. But an apparition of an older woman with her hair done up in a bun has been seen, and it's suspected to be Mrs. Deane.

After its time as a Mountie residence, it was repurposed into a rooming house, where reports of violence were commonplace. Among the most infamous incidents is a murder-suicide that allegedly took place within its walls on March 25, 1971, fueling speculation that some spirits have never left. The victims, according to Ian Gibbs in *Calgary's Most Haunted*, were Irma and Roderick Umpherville.

The City of Calgary purchased the building, turning it into a community arts space called the Dandelion Gallery. Then, in 1978, they gave it a Historic Resource designation. It was during its time as a gallery that the ghost stories began to circulate. Visitors and staff have reported disembodied laughter, shades on the main stairs, a pipe-smoking man where Deane's study used to be, the spectre of a sad, dark-haired woman in another room, and a bloodstain in an upstairs closet that just won't go away, no matter how hard you scrub.

The Deane House also has the reputation of crying wolf, according to Gibbs. The alarm system has been known to go off repeatedly. Property managers have often been pulled out of bed in the middle of the night to head down to the house, now a restaurant, and discover nothing is afoot.

As to what draws Smith to the allure of folklore and ghastly tales, it's all about the uncanny.

When asked why she has had such a prolific career, she admitted she always wanted to write, and she has always had an interest in the paranormal — ever since her father, Gordon Hunter, told her about the ghost that haunted the Bank of Montreal building in downtown Toronto. Of course, that was in the 1950s, and that institution is now home to another Canadian institution: the Hockey Hall of Fame.

When I interviewed her for the Superstitious Times back then, she admitted being in awe.

"My father said, in passing, 'They say there's a ghost in there,'" Smith recalled. "My little jaw just dropped and I was tormenting him with questions. "He didn't know anything about it. He didn't know he would start this storm inside," she added. "I've loved that story ever since. It's so poignant and it's so verifiable."[4]

"I can't come up with a better phrase than 'It's the history and the mystery,'" she said, during our Zoom call. "I love social history and I have written other books on social history, *Great Canadian Love Stories, Great Canadian Romances* … the mystery."

There's a personal connection for Smith too. She lost her husband, Bob, in 2022, but she continued to feel his presence after his passing. Comforting signs followed her and changed her perspective on what happens when we finally leave this plane of existence. "The first three nights after he died, I could hear him walking down the hall and stopping in at the main bathroom. That was his routine. I would go to bed first, so he would use the main bathroom, to not disturb me," she recalled. "And then last summer … yellow butterflies were all over the place. They would fly in front of me and stop and do little dances around my face."

She drew a connection between the butterflies and her husband. Ghost stories are enormously important to Smith. And the oldest story, Smith recalled, involves Viking ships in L'Anse aux Meadows. In both Placentia Bay and L'Anse aux Meadows, witnesses have reported seeing Viking longships coming to shore.

"That's who we were," she admitted of ghost stories. "That's our past social history and that is extraordinarily important.

"It's such a huge country and I think it's extraordinarily important because what Canada is, is the people," Smith added. "We can't forget them."

✦

There's another story about the hauntings of the Banff Springs Hotel that I'd like to share with you. Like many other tourists driving through the mountains, my parents decided to spend a bit of time in the Rockies. Although they stayed in Canmore — just a twenty-minute drive away from the Banff Springs Hotel — the mystique of the mountains called them. It wasn't just the fabulous that attracted us. Like Jasper Park Lodge, the Banff Springs Hotel — a grand, Gothic structure — was built by the Canadian Pacific Railway to cater to those travelling the railway. Tourists aren't the only ones who seem to like these hotels. Spirits seem to find them attractive too, and what's a Gothic building without a few resident spirits — and not of the alcoholic variety?

I would return to Banff some twenty years later with my brother when he lived in Calgary. My brother and I cut through the building to make it to the back patio that overlooks the Bow River. We goofed around and took in the awe-inspiring view. Even in our twenties, though, it was the mysterious spirits that inhabited the hotel that really interested me. I mentioned the Ghost Bride to my brother, but he is not a ghost person. I remember trying to get him to watch a horror movie, and he said, "Nope."

The Ghost Bride is the most famous ghostly legend associated with the Fairmont Banff Springs Hotel. Her story has grown beyond the confines of the hotel and was even featured on Canada Post's Haunted Canada postage stamp series. While I previously mentioned that she has been seen in the Rob Roy dining room, the origins of her ghostly presence — and how she came to be forever dancing in the afterlife — vary depending on the source.

The most common version of the legend dates back to the 1920s or 1930s, when a young bride was set to celebrate her wedding in a grand hotel. As she descended the hotel's grand spiral staircase, tragedy struck. Some accounts claim that the hem of her long, flowing gown caught on a candle's flame. Panicked and disoriented, she stumbled and fell down the staircase, suffering a fatal injury — some say she broke her neck upon impact. Others suggest she tripped on her gown or veil in a moment of nervous excitement, leading to the same tragic end.

Since her death, guests and hotel staff have reported eerie sightings of a ghostly bride in a white gown. She is often seen gliding through the hotel's corridors, appearing on the grand staircase, or even dancing alone in the ballroom as if living out her wedding day without tragedy.

Despite the tragic circumstances of her passing, the Ghost Bride is not believed to be a malevolent spirit. Rather, she remains a sorrowful yet graceful presence, forever tied to the Banff Springs Hotel — one of Canada's most historic and haunted landmarks — and a reminder of the tired, forlorn bride trope that afflicts Canadian ghost stories.

One of the most common ghost stories across Canada is the forlorn bride-to-be. You'll see it in Ontario, you'll see it in New Brunswick, and you see it here in Alberta. It's almost as if every person who read *Wuthering Heights* found it necessary to include their own Catherine Earnshaw on the property.

Hotels and other buildings aren't the only place you'll find spirits. Canada is a country of the great outdoors, and some of the activities that humans engage in out in the wild are dangerous. So, it's not uncommon in places with heavy mining, like Sudbury or Cobalt, in Ontario, that the ghosts of miners have been seen. Alberta's Atlas Coal Mine is one of these touchstones of our mining industry's past.

A 2009 *Globe and Mail* article[5] featured the apparitions that have been sighted at the national historic landmark. In particular, the wife of one of the employees is said to revisit the manager's office that she rushed to one day. She heard an explosion, and it is alleged that when she shared her experience with the manager, he went down in the mine to investigate. That is where he met his end. Staff members keep the manager's door bolted out of respect these days.

Pretty Alice is another spirit that tends to stay close to her working quarters: a brass bed in the attic. Not much is said about Alice, but people have reported seeing an orb of light there. During the peak of the coal mine, Drumheller Valley was full of bars and brothels. Pretty Alice was one of many women offering a warm bed to miners.

There are more stories of macabre death, including that of a union organizer who died after he had a run-in with mining "special constables." With so much death, from both disasters and politics, it's no wonder the confines of the building hold in that energy.

Sometimes a place will seem haunted, even if there's no particular spirit that can be identified. Turtle Mountain is one of those places. On April 29, 1903, a landslide on Turtle Mountain in southern Alberta, then part of the North-West Territories, wiped out the mining community of Frank. Between seventy to ninety people lost their lives at 4:10 a.m.

The cause of the landslide isn't known. It's not surprising that one occurred, though, as the region sits on the Turtle Mountain Thrust fault. So, the go-to cause was an earthquake. But some have suggested that the landslide might have been the result of a distant volcanic eruption or even a weakening of the mountain due to coal mining. Canadian country and folk singer Stompin' Tom Connors wrote the song "How the Mountain Came Down" as an homage to the disaster.

Why would a natural disaster fall under the category of the uncanny? It's mostly the eerie feeling that people have when visiting the place. Witnesses have reported seeing apparitions and phantom lights walking along the debris field.

Death can occur anywhere, but more people die in hospitals than in other places. It's not surprising, then, that they have more than their fair share of ghosts. Some have more than others.

The Charles Camsell Hospital in Edmonton was originally built by Jesuits in 1914. It was operated by them until 1942, when the American Army purchased it to use as a staging ground while they built the Alaska Highway. By 1944, with the war almost over, they sold it to the Albertan government, who after much coaxing, turned it into a tuberculosis treatment facility for Indigenous patients from Alberta and the Territories.

Edmontonians who live in the neighbourhood of Inglewood sometimes refer to the Camsell Hospital as the haunted hospital. Given the fact that Indigenous people were patients, it's not a big stretch that there was some neglect, and since the hospital, like most healthcare institutions, served as a teaching hospital, there was plenty of experimentation done on the patients — experimentation that was often painful and usually done without their consent.

In *Eerie Edmonton*, paranormal researcher Rhonda Parrish noted that there are still family members looking for the bodies of loved ones who were treated at the hospital. In late 2021, Indigenous groups were heard and the grounds of Camsell were dug up in the search for bodies.[6]

Still, the revenants of a troubled past have been seen and heard on the property. Shadows of people have been seen in the walls; loud footsteps have been heard in the halls by investigators and urban explorers.

Alberta is full of plenty of ghostly stories, some pre-dating its existence as a Canadian province, and others during its dawn. The MacKay Avenue School, in Edmonton, is a perfect example of a haunted location tied to the government, as the first sessions of Parliament happened within those walls.

✦

Morgan Knudsen co-founded Entityseeker Paranormal Research & Teachings with her friend Stephanie Wertz, who passed away in 2011. I've spoken with Kundsen multiple times over the years about her challenges as an investigator in Edmonton. The first time we chatted was when I covered the premiere of *Paranormal 9-1-1* when Knudsen was a subject matter expert.

Knudsen didn't know when she co-founded Entityseeker that she was following in the footsteps of her great-great-grandfather, Dr. Albert Durrant Watson, who was the president of the Association for Psychical Research of Canada in 1918.

Watson was a poet, physician, astronomer, and psychical researcher. He was born on January 8, 1859, in Dixie (modern-day Mississauga), Upper Canada. He became known for his psychical research and séances with medium Louis Benjamin.

It all began when Watson's friends asked him if they could use the back room in his Toronto home for a séance. They told him that they wanted to conduct a séance with a man named Louis Benjamin. They told him that he was a "channeler," Knudsen recalled. "A.D. was skeptical, especially when he learned that Benjamin had at most a Grade 4 education. His friends assured him that Benjamin was the real deal — he talked in dialects, sharing information beyond his range of knowledge.

"Now, A.D.'s mother had recently died. Louis didn't know this. [Watson's friends] didn't know this. In the séance, though, Louis turned to him and started talking as A.D.'s mom, coming out with phrases and information [he couldn't have known]. He never knew this woman. This blew A.D.'s mind."

Watson transcribed Louis Benjamin's words. After that, he began a deep dive into a collective of entities called the Humble Ones of the 20th Plane. "The different planes were like different frequencies of thought," Knudsen said. "Different ranges of joy that these entities would exist on."

Benjamin went on to publish two books on the subject: *The Twentieth Plane: A Psychic Revelation* and *Birth Through Death: The Ethics of the Twentieth Plane, A Revelation Received Through the Psychic Consciousness of Louis Benjamin*. Watson would become the president of the Canadian Society for Psychical Research, famous for his paranormal research.

Knudsen's ties to Watson weren't shared with her until later in her life, six years after she started Entityseeker in 2003. It was only after her maternal grandfather died that the information on Watson was disclosed. The fact that it took so long for her to learn of the connection shows, Knudsen told me, that people are hesitant to talk about the paranormal. "They knew what career I was in, and no one said a thing," she said. "There's this wall of censorship, this weird wall; we don't talk about this."

In her experience she's found that this reluctance is much more pronounced in Canada. Knudsen admitted that there is a stark difference between how Canada and the States perceive ghosts.[7]

✦

There are plenty of hauntings across the province. The North Saskatchewan River valley has plenty of inexplicable events such as in Fort Edmonton Park and in the Fairmont Hotel Macdonald. Those tales of hauntings were influenced by people and ideas coming out of Ontario, including Knudsen's great-great-grandfather Dr. Albert Durrant Watson and the Spiritualist movement. But regardless of big-city visitors, the small-town worldview and Christian character of Alberta influence how Alberta processes the paranormal, according to Knudsen. "[Edmonton's] got a very small-town mentality, which is one of the things that drives me insane about living here," she admitted, with a laugh. "Because I don't have that mentality, but you get more hometown Christian, maybe a little bit more religious, but just a little bit simpler in terms of their way of life."

Mind you, the simpler life isn't a bad thing in Edmonton.

"It's just, Alberta has the mentality: 'Well, that's fun to learn about, but no, we don't discuss it,'" she said.

She once investigated a community forty-five minutes outside of Edmonton with cryptid sightings. She and her fellow investigators tracked down eyewitnesses, but when she sat down with people, they wouldn't talk. "You hit a wall here, really fast," Knudsen said. But the interest is still there. Knudsen performs live shows and they're always sold out. "It's not that people don't want to learn. They do want to learn. They want to explore it. But they don't want to make it about them," she said. "There's a limit. We want to hear about it, but that's as far as it goes."

Josh Turner had Knudsen on his show *Paranormal Round Table* and admitted the sentiments of Canadians whenever they called into his show. Many would share their stories with him, but the moment they were asked to be on the show, go on record or state their name, there was silence and more than likely a polite "No thank you."

Much like the weather currents being unable to go over the mountains, the paranormal beliefs also get left on one side of the mountains. Alberta has a different feel to it, as opposed to British Columbia. But that's not surprising, because they are two different provinces.

As for the Territories, Knudsen has more sources in Alaska than in Canada's Great White North. But there are more than just polar bears, musk oxen, and glaciers there.

5

Saskatchewan

Saskatchewan has a newfound place in my heart, as I learned recently that my paternal grandfather was born in Fenwood, Saskatchewan, to immigrant German parents who left Lutsk, Ukraine, to start a new life in Canada's Prairies. History is pretty neat, especially when you learn more about the journeys of your own path.

That's what historian Kristin Catherwood did in her hometown of Radville. The supernatural is a topic that is near and dear to Catherwood, though, oddly, she is an admitted skeptic and leans into agnosticism when it comes to any spiritual or religious background. Still, she finds the paranormal intensely interesting, and she has spent a lot of time exploring stories of the unknown and the people who share them.

Catherwood cites writer of paranormal history Jo-Anne Christensen as a big part of her childhood interest in the paranormal. "I do wonder what role the internet has in shaping belief or reinforcing belief or just connecting believers with other believers or what because I remember being a kid and being fascinated by the ghosts and the paranormal," she recalled, adding that in the early days of web browsing she would read the stories on websites like Shadow Lands.

She developed, wrote, and led the Haunted History Tour in Radville for seven years. "I was a summer student at the museum in town, and I developed that," she recalled. "Leading that tour for seven years, I learned a lot about what people respond to, as well as collecting all these stories," she said, adding that in her job at Heritage Saskatchewan, issues around belief would often come up.

Many people approached Catherwood after her workshops and spoke to her one-on-one about their experiences. Her Radville tour grew and expanded thanks to the stories shared by those who came out during the summer months.

"People would invariably make a point to come to me after, not during. And the same thing with the tour people," Catherwood recalled. "There would be some brave, more extroverted people who'd say, 'Let me tell you a story' in the middle of the tour, but usually, they'd kind of sidle up to me during the tour, or they'd hang back and come and tell me this story."

She collected the stories people told her. "I always told people 'I'm not going to share who is telling these stories. You're an anonymous source,'" she said. It seems that is one of the most Canadian things people want when it comes to the paranormal: anonymity. They don't want to be identified as someone who claims to have had contact with the paranormal.

"Sometimes people would guess because it's a small town. And sometimes people were like, 'That's my story.'" Still, the most common response from those she has collected stories from is "Please, don't tell anyone."

The ghost walks were consistently popular in Radville, something Catherwood attributes to the fact that she stayed true to the heritage and folklore in the community. Although some suggested she arrange jump scares and other elements of pop culture horror, Catherwood always shot that down.

Her tour attracted members of the local television show *Knights of the Dark*, who visited Radville to explore the allegedly haunted hospital, which was torn down in 2017, three years after she began running the tour. "I was interviewed a few times about it," she said. "It was something that drew a lot of interest."

Catherwood admits that she isn't the go-to for Saskatchewan ghost stories. But that's where Jo-Anne Christensen, John Robert Colombo, and Barbara Smith come into play.

Two of the biggest ghost stories in Saskatchewan involve what's called "the St. Louis Light" and the Moosehead Inn in Kenosee Lake. Unfortunately, the Moosehead burned to the ground in September 2021.[1]

Iconic enough to have been immortalized on a Canada Post stamp, the St. Louis Light is tied to Saskatchewan's railway history. Just a few miles north of the small Prairie town, on your way to Prince Albert, is a flat patch of earth on which railway tracks once ran. The best place for sighting the Light is one kilometre west along Donnybrook Road, according to users on Reddit.

As with any legend, the origin story has been altered, tweaked, or embellished to suit the public's desire for the dramatic. Christensen wrote about the Light, mentioning that it was one of four things local residents hold dear. The other three items are the Métis leaders Louis Riel and Gabriel Dumont, and the hockey players who made it to the National Hockey League. Defenseman Rich Pilon is the biggest name, and Joey Tetarenko is the other player since Christensen's book came out in 1995.

Christensen notes that the phenomenon is still observed, and its story has been shared through the generations.

> The apparition is unfailingly described as a huge beam of white light, reminiscent of the headlights on old-fashioned trains. It follows the land as the tracks once did and has been seen approaching St. Louis by hundreds of witnesses over the years, including the village's mayor. Many people offer their own personal accounts of the light, as well as stories handed down to them by their parents and grandparents. Naturally, with these stories come popular theories regarding the origin of the beacon.[2]

✦

Most of those stories feature a conductor or engineer who quite literally lost his head in a bad accident that happened while he was performing a routine check of the tracks. The story focuses on the spirit looking for his head. Some believe that the light is a sign that the conductor still seeks his head.

Others believe that the light is from a lantern held by a man who is signalling the trains to switch tracks. But, as Christensen noted, the height of the light isn't right. It's too high to be a lantern held by a man walking along the tracks. A more reasonable theory is that the light is a psychic imprint of the train that came through the area regularly.

Christensen shared the funny story of Chris McLeod, who on one occasion, when he was a teenager, parked his car along where the tracks used to run. Rumour has it that people run into various issues with their cars when they play daredevil with the phantom train. They are unable to start the vehicle or the windshield wipers go off on their own. Unfortunately for McLeod, his alternator caught fire. McLeod, instead of trying to find ways of putting out the fire, booted it all the way back to Prince Albert at 120 kilometres per hour.

Don MacPhedran, a volunteer at the Prince Albert Historical Museum, tried to debunk the phenomenon in a letter to the editor in the *Prince Albert Daily Herald*. "The lights are vehicle lights that appear and then disappear owing to the changes in the elevation of the highway. They are plainly visible with a high-power telephoto lens or a good field glass," he wrote.[3]

But St. Louis residents scoffed at his theory. Some even wrote into the paper telling their side of the story. One resident said that their great-grandmother would see the lights when she was a teenager. And that was before the advent of cars.

✦

As I mentioned, the Moosehead Inn unfortunately burned down in 2021, but in its day, it was a popular place. Bands like Loverboy and Harlequin performed there, and the place was hopping.

Dale Orsted bought the property in 1989 and began renovating the place. As soon as renovations began, the haunting started too. Orsted and his girlfriend reported loud banging and footsteps and noted that items would go missing throughout the building. But most of the activity was centred on the cabaret. Eventually, paranormal investigators Roy Bauer and Chris Rutkowski investigated the location. Bauer theorized that the original owner, Archibald Grandison, was not too happy with the changes. Whoever the spectre is, they were still active up until the fire of 2021. In an article written about the fire, Orsted acknowledged the ghost, saying his staff investigated a loud bang in the cabaret.[4]

✦

If you drive west from Kenosee, you'll discover another haunt with spirited guests: the Hopkins Dining Parlour in Moose Jaw. The restaurant, which was featured in the TV series *Creepy Canada* in 2003, is named for the family that built the house the restaurant is in: Edward and Minnie Hopkins.

The Hopkins Dining Parlour's founder and former owner, Gladys Pierce, believes that the Hopkins, although they are long gone physically, didn't exactly leave. She believes that they have stuck around. The kitchen, in particular, has been home to some paranormal activity. Frying pans have been thrown across the room, cooks have felt someone tapping on their shoulders, and other staff have felt their tense muscles being massaged.

In the main dining area, apparitions of a woman's single shoe or the fleeting hem of a skirt have been seen, and candles on the tables have mysteriously been lit on their own.[5]

✦

My favourite ghost story from Saskatchewan was not covered by Christensen, Smith, or Colombo. It involves happenings in the Centennial Market in Regina. The building was thrust into existence in 1918 in the provincial capital's Warehouse District. Built by the Eaton family for their retail store, it housed the Eaton's department store until the 1980s, when Sears took over the space. They vacated the premises in 2017, and up until its permanent closure in May 2024, the Centennial Market served as a marketplace for independent retailers.

The market, which has been featured in stories appearing on CBC, Global, and the Superstitious Times website, has got all the fixings of a Nancy Drew caper, including hidden rooms, phantom footsteps, malfunctioning elevators, and the lurid details of people taking their own lives. (Well, the original Nancy Drew stories may not include incidents of suicide, but in the 2019 TV series with Kennedy McMann in the titular role, Nancy is haunted by the ghost of her mother, who, depressed, had died by suicide soon after giving birth to Nancy.)

Deborah Mathias is an admitted channeller, or clairsentient; she can pick up the emotions lingering in places. She told me she heard spirits all the time in the building back in 2019. They even uncovered a secret room they called the CEO's office.

Paranormal investigations were conducted by Cory Nagy and his team, SOTG Paranormal Research Saskatchewan. He told me that they conducted experiments in the CEO's office, where a record player had been observed switching on by itself. Both he and fellow investigator Matthew Lay heard footsteps running up the stairs to the room, scaring them.[6] They also had a psychic working with them and they seemed to believe that a young woman was killed when the freight elevator crushed her.

I asked Catherwood about the attention the market has received, and she admitted that there may be some change in how Canadians respond to incidents of the paranormal. "I don't know if there's been a bit of a shift, and if that is aligned with there being so many paranormal shows on TV," Catherwood commented.

"People are super interested in this but are a little cautious about talking about it publicly," Catherwood added. "I went into doing the research for that tour thinking people were going to be more reticent than they actually were."

She believes that more and more, people are looking at hauntings with a nod to historical issues. "There's the paranormal and then there's these really difficult histories that are starting to come up more. You see this in the States, where stories about slavery are being told more."

The same trend is happening in Canada, where we have talked more about the history of Indigenous realities in Canada, including the topics of residential schools and the Sixties Scoop.

"Ghost stories and the paranormal can be a way to deal with some of the darker sides of history," she admitted. "Making it something beyond human can help tell that story or deal with it. Again, that's just a theory."

The ghost stories Catherwood shares on her Radville tour form only a small part of the tour. Along her walk, she also focuses on topics like colonialism, racism, violence, alcoholism, and mental illness.

"[I talk about things] that weren't generally talked about in our cozy community history books, or the sort of institutionalized histories of our provinces and the country as a whole. [Those usually present pretty sanitized stories of] settlement, progress, pioneers, and these achievements and gloss over the social harms that occurred in the process," Catherwood added. "Once the paranormal is there, you could delve into those darker histories and reflect on it a little bit more. The ghost made an accessible entryway."

Ghost stories can serve as vehicles for sharing the past. Our history, as taught in our classrooms, is usually pretty dry. It often focuses on the political or economic. It's a story of settlement, colonialism, and nation-building. It's also exclusionary. Ghost stories feature all kinds of people — young and old, male and female, rich and poor, Black, Indigenous, Asian. The fact that they offer some entertainment, too, helps to soften the blow of our dark history.

"It's community building in a way," Catherwood admitted. "When you know those local ghost stories, are you a part of the community? It's a way to talk about what the official narrative of our history leaves out: those very human stories, because ghosts, as much as they imply the past, also imply a person — an actual human being who did something."

6

Manitoba

Ghost stories are important to historian and writer Matthew Komus. The Winnipeg native stressed that they help connect people to places (and to where they are). Komus knows Manitoba well. And even better, he knows the province's ghost stories. Outside of Barbara Smith's and John Robert Colombo's books covering all of Canada, Komus is the only Manitoba-specific writer who has captured the lurid tales.

There are plenty of ghost stories, and some of Canada's most violent moments happened during the Red River Rebellion. The subsequent execution of rebellion leader Louis Riel is one of the most significant events in Canadian history. The narrative around Riel has changed over time, thankfully, but that history does find its way into the spectral tales around the areas of Manitoba.

Still, the first known ghost stories surfaced in Manitoba when settlers entered the province in 1870, the year Manitoba entered Confederation. Fifteen years later, after the Canadian government mismanaged its promise to provide the Métis with 1.4 million acres of land, the Red River Resistance entered centre stage.

Most of these tales, Komus admitted, are associated with Upper and Lower Fort Garry. Lower Fort Garry is northeast of Winnipeg, just before you hit Selkirk on the way to Lake Winnipeg. Lower Fort Garry was a bit of a quagmire it seems, and the philandering governor, George Simpson, used the flooding of Upper Fort Garry in 1826 as a pretext for building the lower fort in 1831. Simpson, who is suspected of having thirteen children with eight different Métis or Indigenous women, got married to his British cousin Frances Simpson and they moved to Lower Fort Garry in 1832. (Old George didn't want to run into any of his exes or lovers in Winnipeg.)

After the death of their first-born son, the Simpsons fled the fort life for England. The fort would be completed by 1847, thanks to the man Simpson left in charge of building it, Pierre LeBlanc. It's the spirit of LeBlanc, among others, that is suspected of haunting Lower Fort Garry.[1]

The reason his restless spirit is said to make its presence known is his tragic end. He was a talented building manager, and his employer, the Hudson's Bay Company, required his services for Fort Vancouver, which was located on the Columbia River just north of modern Portland, Oregon.

LeBlanc packed up his wife, Nancy, and their four children, and they made their way to Fort Assiniboine, north of Edmonton. Two days after their departure, LeBlanc's eldest daughter died. She was buried along the Athabasca River.

As they progressed west, they ran into issues while traversing the Dalles des Morts, or Death Rapids, in the area of Lake Revelstoke. The rapids no longer exist on maps because the Revelstoke Dam, constructed in 1984, flooded them out.

The canoe LeBlanc and his family were in struck a rock in the rapids and began to take on water. In a panic, LeBlanc jumped ship. His body would never be recovered, nor would the bodies of his three other children.

As for the haunting of the fort, well, it's hard not to find a structure in there that isn't haunted. The Ross Cottage is suspected of being haunted by a young girl with tuberculosis who was placed there. The Fur Loft is said to have poltergeist activity, as well as the apparition of a man sleeping on the furs. When a security guard asked the man to leave, he turned and walked through the wall.

The Big House has a basement that no one wants to set foot in. At one point, it was a bar, and it was in that establishment that a man drank himself to death after he learned his wife was leaving him. His spirit haunts the space still.

The Warehouse, which was opened as a penitentiary in 1871, had a turnkey (corrections officer) named Thomas Slack. Much like every man in Manitoba during those times, he had a country wife (a Métis or Indigenous common-law partner). Well, he had received a letter from his wife back in England saying that she was going to move with the kids to Canada. Now, that wouldn't have been as big of a problem if it weren't for the fact the letter was delayed and she was due in Manitoba in the next couple of days.

There's no paper trail, but it is said that Slack walked up to the third floor and took his life. These days, people working at the fort will feel like they are being watched, and some have seen the figure of a man looking down at them from a third-floor window.

The last building within the walls of the fort is the Blacksmith's Shop, which featured prominently in a 2012 episode of *Ghost Hunters International*. A reconstruction of the original building was made by Parks Canada in 1971. One of the original buildings had been destroyed by an explosion. During Victoria Day celebrations in 1877, someone made fireworks and stored them in the blacksmith's shop. This poor decision didn't pan out well, as can be expected, as the fireworks blew up, injuring many and killing at least one child.[2] It is said that even on days when there aren't any re-enactments happening, people can still hear the bellows going and the anvil being struck.

Not only are there spectres within the walls of the fort, there have been sightings outside the walls too.

In 1903, a member of the 12th Manitoba Dragoons witnessed a man and a woman coming down the road in an ox-drawn Red River cart. The cart made no sound, which was unusual. The carts were made of wood; thus, they were loud. The cart would pass by several times until the guard told them to halt.

Naturally, the cart vanished.

Komus uncovered a more recent story involving a University of Manitoba student who, on her way home to Selkirk, had to quickly steer off the highway to avoid hitting a man standing in the middle of the road. She thought she had hit the man, but upon investigating, she found the car to be undamaged and the surrounding area free of any human-sized roadkill. The woman got back into her car and started driving again. When she looked in the rearview mirror, she saw a man staring back at her. He had dark eyes, stubble, and long scraggly hair. He also wore a felt hat. His visage disappeared once she reached the northern part of the fort.

It was not an isolated incident.

Every time the woman travelled by the fort, she saw the man in her rearview mirror. It became so consistent that she would avoid driving along Provincial Trunk Highway 9 just so she wouldn't see the man.

Komus wasn't always into collecting these ghost stories. His interest in ghosts was entirely accidental. He was a guide for various tours in Winnipeg's Exchange District. His chief focus was architecture, but the most common question he got for a location was, "Is it haunted?"

"I was always getting these ghost questions, so I saw that there was an interest and started doing the research," he recalled, adding he started his ghost tour fifteen years ago.

The Fort Garry Hotel is a popular spot on his tours. A grand ball was hosted by the hotel when it opened on December 10, 1913, and it seems that one couple had such a good time at the ball that they decided to never leave. To this day, a man and woman in old-timey party outfits have been seen on the upper floors of the hotel.

Still, the floor of note in the hotel is the second floor. Room 202 comes up in multiple reports as being the cold spot, as it were. Guests have reported stolen property, the opening and closing of the closet doors, and rattling door handles. They've even woken up in the middle of the night to someone sitting on the end of the bed or even crawling into bed with them. One gentleman reported seeing a ball of green light floating down the hallway and entering through the door of the room he was to stay in.

Many of the people who have experienced these things have decided to cut short their stays.

Room 202 even has the delightful occurrence of a reappearing bloodstain that staff loathe having to clean up. It's reported that the hotel has changed the carpets in the room in the past, yet the stain keeps coming back.

The story that Komus uncovered in his book was that a newlywed couple stayed in Room 202. The new bride, excited to begin her new life, came down with a bad headache. Her husband, being the dapper chap he was, went to fetch her some pills. She went to lie down on the bed, and when she awoke, she discovered it was later than she thought. Her beau had not returned. A hotel staff member knocked on her door to inform her that her husband had been killed in a car accident.

The woman would lock herself in her room and take her life in Room 202's closet.

A common thread connecting all haunted hotels across the country is that of the forlorn bride or wife. Similar stories are connected to the Banff Springs Hotel, to the location of the former Queen's Royal Hotel, on Niagara-on-the-Lake, and to the Algonquin Resort in Saint Andrews, New Brunswick. People love a good Victorian romance tale, and Canada serves up plenty.

So, the Fort Garry Hotel is another example of this trope. However, there's a pretty substantial case that got media coverage from the hotel. During a federal Liberal Party caucus retreat to Winnipeg in 2000, MP Brenda Chamberlain told *The Globe and Mail* about her experience in Room 202.[3]

The MP switched rooms after something slipped into bed beside her, not once but twice in the same night. "The close encounter clearly unnerved the self-proclaimed skeptic of the paranormal, so much so that she switched rooms and says she would not stay at the hotel again," the reporter wrote.

If anyone inquires, the hotel will assure its guests that the stories about Room 202 are "just speculation" or "before our time." The only other confirmed account of a bizarre encounter comes from the current owner, Ida Albo, who once saw a doppelgänger — the ghostly double of a living person. This occurred in Room 528, where she saw the apparition of her husband, whom she had just argued with.[4]

Although historic locations like Lower Fort Garry and city centre haunts like the Fort Garry Hotel have easily accessible ghost stories, there were parts of Manitoba that Komus wanted to find representative stories about. However, their culture presented a challenge for him.

"Southern Manitoba tends to be fairly conservative religiously, and there are few stories from that part of the province," he said, adding that the Interlake region of Manitoba provided him with a wealth of ghost stories in part due to the community's Icelandic roots.

Throughout his collection of stories, the one that resonated the most with him was related to the Walker Theatre. It's been known as the Burton Cummings Theatre since 2002 as an homage to Guess Who frontman and Winnipeg native Burton Cummings. It's also colloquially known as The Burt.

The Walker Theatre was opened on February 18, 1907, and it hosted many iconic figures from the entertainment world like Charlie Chaplin, Louis Armstrong, Groucho Marx, Bob Hope, and Harry Houdini. But it also played a role in social change. Harriet Walker was an early suffragette who helped Nellie McClung host her first Women's Parliament at the Walker. Manitoba would be the first province to allow women to vote, on January 28, 1916.

What makes The Burt spooky are a couple of stories. The expensive seats in the theatre, "The Gods," give a vibe of phantom audience members. Sometimes, when performers are practising on the stage, they hear applause coming from "The Gods."

Dramatist and novelist Laurence Irving and his wife, Mabel Hackney, wrapped up their final show *The Importance of Being Earnest* at the Walker and then boarded the *Empress of Ireland*. That would be the last thing they would do, as Canada's worst peacetime maritime disaster would happen on May 29, 1914. A total of 1,012 people died, including Irving and Hackney. A plaque was placed in the lobby of the Walker Theatre, honouring their memory. It is suspected the two have returned to the last theatre they performed at.

There is one more presence at The Burt/Walker: Joe the Box Office Attendant. It seems the man has decided that he wanted his own curtain call. He worked for the Walkers until the First World War came calling. The Military Service Act of 1917 forced men aged twenty to forty-five into military service.

Joe trained in England and fought on the front lines in France. It was there that he was exposed to mustard gas. Joe survived, but he came back to

Winnipeg in a weakened state. He would later contract pneumonia and died not long after his return home.

"The ghosts are supposed to be putting on their final show over and over. They died tragically," Komus said of Irving and Hackney. "Nowadays, no one has a clue who they are, but at the time, they were really well known, and the fact that the theatre is still functioning, with the plaque in their memory, is still on the wall, so I think that one is cool."

Over one hundred years have passed but there's still that connection to place. That's important to a historian like Komus, who admitted to approaching each story with an interest in the storytelling.

"In some ways, I don't fully believe it, but I also don't fully disbelieve in it," he said. "I've had a couple of weird things happen."

One location, Winnipeg's oldest house, Seven Oaks, offered Komus some interesting experiences when he visited. "We heard some strange things at Seven Oaks, and we weren't even on a ghost investigation," he said, adding he worked there as a University of Manitoba student in 2002. "We would hear footsteps. We would hear sounds of things breaking and nothing would be there."

Another site of paranormal fascination, one that dates back to the heyday of the Spiritualist movement in the early twentieth century, is the Hamilton House in Winnipeg. The site is widely believed to be haunted.

Dr. Thomas Glendenning Hamilton compiled a collection of parapsychological data during his lifetime, from 1873 to 1935. All the materials were donated to the university's library between 1979 and 1986.

Hamilton was born in Agincourt, Ontario, and lived there for ten years until his family moved to Saskatchewan. After his father passed away, Hamilton moved to Manitoba.

He attended séances and studied a medium by the name of Elizabeth M. That began in 1922, and he presented his findings to the public in April 1926.[5]

"There was so much Spiritualism stuff that I never even got into the house," Komus admitted. "What I found interesting is how mainstream Spiritualism was. These weren't people on the fringes of society. [Hamilton] was one of the most respected doctors in the city."

Barbara Smith noted in her book *Great Canadian Ghost Stories* that even actor Dan Aykroyd's great-grandfather, Samuel, held séances at Hamilton's house.

"Dr. Hamilton became determined to scientifically prove whether or not communication with the dead was possible," Smith wrote. "He strove to keep his paranormal experiments as scientifically rigorous as possible. Toward that end, he invited a photographer to be present during the séances."[6]

Even Sherlock Holmes creator Sir Arthur Conan Doyle and Prime Minister William Lyon Mackenzie King visited the house at 185 Kelvin Street, now known as Henderson Highway. Unfortunately, the site is in a state of flux as party shop Gags Unlimited put the property up for sale in September 2024. Gags Unlimited, fittingly, sold ghost-hunting equipment like Para4ce Teddy Pods and digital voice recorders.[7]

Hamilton House remains one of Manitoba's most famous haunted locations, but it is far from the only one. The province has a rich supernatural history, with the Fort Garry Hotel's Room 202, Manitoba's first forts, and the Burton Cummings Theatre all standing as reminders of the province's ghostly legacy.

7

The North

Between 1870 and 1880, Britain transferred to Canada what was known as Rupert's Land, along with the North-West Territories and the Arctic Islands. With the addition of these massive tracts of land, Canada was transformed from a small nation of a few colonies to a giant that spanned North America from the Atlantic to the Pacific, and from the 49th parallel to the Arctic Ocean. From this new territory, the Prairie provinces and Canada's northern territories would be created, and with it, the areas of the provinces of Ontario and Quebec would be increased significantly.

Most Canadians don't know much about the North, with the exception, perhaps, that the doomed Franklin expedition was lost on the Arctic Ocean trying to find the Northwest Passage. The story of the doomed crew was immortalized forever in Dan Simmons's historical horror novel *The Terror*, which was made into a TV series starring Jared Harris. It may be that most Canadians don't know all of this, but I find it fascinating because I'm a history nerd and horror hound, and archaeology was my undergrad major at university. It also helps that my brother was an RCMP officer stationed first in Iqaluit and then in Arviat.

A little more historical trivia: The price for the territories was an affordable $1.5 million. Yukon Territory became its own territory in 1898. (In

1999 Nunavut was carved out of the Northwest Territories to become a separate territory.)

The Yukon saw early settlement in the years from 1896 to 1899 thanks to the Klondike Gold Rush that saw approximately one hundred thousand would-be miners flood the area looking for riches. The frontier towns of Whitehorse and Dawson City were established during this time.

Of course, humans had been living in the territories for thousands of years before the arrival of the white settlers. Indigenous groups in the Yukon include the Nahanni, Teslin, Tutchone, Tagish, Gwich'in, and the Inuit. The spiritual beliefs of these groups form the bedrock for all of the paranormal happenings that followed the arrival of whites.

John Robert Colombo shared as an example of such beliefs the account of Igjugarjuk, who was befriended by Danish explorer Knud Rasmussen during his fifth Thule expedition from 1921–24. Igjugarjuk's spiritual journey involved sacrifice; he had to adhere to many of the taboos or proscriptions of what was allowed within Inuit life.[1]

Igjugarjuk had the dream of becoming an *angakkuq* or Inuit medicine man. While pursuing his goal, he experienced a vision of his helping spirit that was sent to him by Pinga, the inland Inuit goddess of the hunt and medicine. She is similar to the coastal Inuit goddess Sedna, the mother of sea mammals. She is also considered a psychopomp, or guardian, who receives the souls of the recently deceased.

> Only toward the end of the thirty days did a helping spirit come to me, a lovely and beautiful helping spirit, whom I had never thought of; it was a white woman; she came to me whilst I had collapsed, exhausted and was sleeping. But still, I saw her lifelike, hovering over me, and from that day I could not close my eyes or dream without seeing her. There is this remarkable thing about my helping spirit, that I have never seen her while awake, but only in dreams. She came to me from Pinga and was a sign that Pinga had not noticed me and would give me powers that would make me a shaman.

Igjugarjuk's spiritual journey to become the shaman for his village took him over a year. He lived for thirty days in a tiny igloo and lived off two sips of water a day. Another shaman, Aua, told Rasmussen in 1922 that the Inuit do not believe, they fear. And thus deities like Pinga and Sedna were to be revered.[2]

The Inuit stories of shamanism, cosmology, and deities like Sedna were gradually supplanted by those of the Europeans who started settling in areas like Whitehorse, Yellowknife, and Iqaluit (formerly Frobisher Bay). The spirit stories of the Inuit have fortunately never been forgotten, but the infusion of more traditional Victorian-flavoured stories became more prominent in the North from the late nineteenth century on. Those Victorian tropes include unrequited love, unfinished business, and tragic ends.

Yukon

If you're a complete geography nerd like me, you spend a lot of time looking at random spots around the globe on Google Maps. If you happen to look for the Caribou Hotel in Carcross, Yukon Territory, you'll find a street view shot from 2009. A lot has happened since then, as I learned when I had the chance to chat with one of its current owners, Anne Morgan. She and her husband, Jamie Toole, were renovating the building when their experiences within the walls of the Caribou made them believers in the paranormal.[3] The previous owner, Alice McGuire, who ran the hotel from 1992 to 1998 had similar experiences.

John Firth, a former journalist, wrote *The Caribou Hotel: Hauntings, Hospitality, a Hunter, and the Parrot* in 2019. In the book, he chronicles the stories of Bessie Gideon, one of the former operators of the hotel, and a foul-mouthed parrot named Polly. Both are still very much present.

Polly became a resident of the hotel when his owners, Captain James Alexander and his wife, asked the Gideons to look after the bird while they took a trip on the SS *Princess Sophia*. The Alexanders visited the Caribou every fall and brought with them various pets, including their yellow-naped Amazon parrot, Polly. Unfortunately, on October 25, 1918, the SS *Princess Sophia* sank, and a total of 298 passengers, sixty-five crew, an unknown number of Chinese workers, twenty-five horses, and five dogs died on the ship. The only survivor was an English setter, suspected of belonging to the Alexanders.

People still report seeing the figure of a woman standing in the window with a parrot on her shoulder.

When asked if Yukoners have any issue with sharing their ghost stories, Firth opened up. "People like ghosts. They think they're cool. They may not necessarily believe in them, but they love the stories. If you ask them, they'll admit that they do have a certain amount of fear about them, which is kind of weird."

Some people have had encounters and have unfortunately been "laughed out of the room" because others don't believe them, Firth acknowledged. He says that he doesn't believe people are lying about their experiences. The Whitehorse resident told me that while he himself has never had an encounter with the uncanny, he has a great deal of interest in ghost stories and the paranormal. He was interested enough to decide that he wanted to write a book about the hauntings at the Caribou Hotel. As research for the book, he sat down with McGuire, who died in December 2021. She had a whole file full of accounts of the experiences that she had while running the hotel.

"She thought that one day she might want to write her stories, but she felt that people would laugh at it," Firth said. "That bothered her greatly."

While she shared a few stories, Firth said she was initially quite guarded, reluctant to open up too much. "She said, 'Well, I'm holding back on all the other stuff because I don't want to make it look like I'm a total nutcase,'" he recalled. "Two weeks later, she knocked on my door and handed me the file, saying, 'I've changed my mind. You can have everything.'"

The experiences of Alice McGuire can be read about in Firth's book, but I'd like to share a vivid experience that stands out: how Bessie's spirit became protective of the staff.

One night when McGuire was closing up early, she came across a blond-haired man wearing messy clothes just inside the front door. He seemed unstable, and McGuire realized she was in trouble. She moved into the bar area and stood behind the pool table. The stranger followed her, cutting her off from any escape routes. As he went to approach her, the TV turned on. Both McGuire and the stranger were perplexed. The TV needed to be turned on manually.

After a few minutes, it turned off on its own, and the man resumed his pursuit.

The TV turned on again with the volume louder. The man noticed that McGuire didn't have a remote and he hesitated. After the TV came on a third time, with the volume turned up as loud as it would go, the man gave up his pursuit and walked out of the hotel. McGuire quickly closed the door and put the security bar in place.

The man stared into the bar for a bit and then got into his vehicle and left. The TV turned off when all signs of danger had abated.

McGuire gave thanks to the emptiness of the bar. "Thank you, whoever you are."

Wanting to add to the stories that McGuire shared with him, Firth visited the hotel to talk to the guests and staff. He found a number who were willing to tell him about their brushes with Bessie and the other ghosts that haunt the place, including the phantom visitors who descend the stairs every October 26.

Unlike most business owners in Canada, Morgan and Toole are more than happy to advertise the hotel's hauntings. "The owners were interested in using the ghost stories to sell the hotel to tourists," Firth said. "Staff and guests were encouraged to share their own stories."

The owners of the Palace Grand Theatre in Dawson are similarly eager to promote their business as a place where people can encounter ghosts. The theatre was originally built in 1899 by American showman and sharpshooter Arizona Charlie (a.k.a. Abram Henson Meadows) and then rebuilt by Parks Canada in the early 1960s to reinvigorate the gold rush history.

"Again, the owners are using the ghosts to try to sell the mystique of the place," Firth said, adding the Parks Canada guides talk about the ghosts they've encountered there. Arizona Charlie could be one of them, as the smell of rosewater emanates from his box in the theatre.

Odd happenings include the lights going on of their own accord and heavy footsteps heard on the third floor. The apparition of a woman is sometimes seen sitting on the sidewalk in front of the Palace Grand.

Firth has spoken to a security guard who mustered the courage to talk about her experiences. "I don't think she was overly enthusiastic initially,"

Firth said. "She said that her training included instructions on what to do if you happen to encounter a spirit. To avoid any such encounters, she talks to each room as she's going through it when she's on her own in the Palace Grand. Firth chuckled a bit about the security guard having to be on guard against ghosts.

Some suspect that the spectre who appears on the sidewalk is Kathleen Eloisa Rockwell, a New York chorus girl who was drawn to the town during the gold rush. Klondike Kate, as she was known, met Alexander Pantages — yes, that Pantages — and the two built the Orpheum Theatre. The enterprise, bankrolled by Rockwell, was successful, but Pantages wanted more, and he left Kate and the Orpheum to pursue greener pastures.

Pantages ended up dying in obscurity. He had to sell off his assets to pay legal fees he incurred trying to defend himself from the charge of raping seventeen-year-old Eunice Pringle. He was found guilty and sentenced to fifty years in prison. Although the sentence was overturned on appeal, his legal struggle cost him his empire. He died in California in 1936, his name only living on through the Hollywood Pantages Theater, home of the Academy Awards ceremony from 1950 to '60.

Of course, the Palace Grand is not the only haunted spot in Dawson. The Westminster Hotel, the Macaulay House, and the Commissioner's Residence are home to spectres of the past who make their presence known by knocks and footsteps. The Macaulay House is typically used by artists in residence for the Klondike Institute of Art and Culture. Some, including Jude Griebel, back in 2017,[4] have shared their experiences for the *Yukon News*.

In the North, ghost stories, such as the ghost ship seen on Lake Laberge, are part of the allure of the gold rush era, but Firth said that he feels the ghost stories are not made up just to attract tourism dollars. There may not be as many stories, but they are an important part of the region's culture, Firth feels. "Our colonial history in the North only dates back about 150 years," he said. "We don't have that longevity of southern Canadian or American communities, who have been around for four hundred years. We don't have the same sort of history or background that would really lend itself to a plethora of ghosts here in the territory."

Northwest Territories

Travel east to the working town of Yellowknife in the Northwest Territories proper, and you'll find ghost stories, too. Not as many as in the Yukon, but they're still there, and some of them, like the Mackenzie River ghost, pre-date the country's formation. Its first European witness, Roderick MacFarlane, who would become the eventual superintendent for the Mackenzie District, witnessed it and shared it in detail.

Augustus Peers was only thirty-three years old when he died on March 15, 1853, at Fort McPherson. His final wish was to be taken to Fort Simpson, which is 890 kilometres as the crow flies. Charles Gaudet would exhume his body in 1859 and take it by dog sled along the Mackenzie River to Fort Good Hope. MacFarlane, Michel Iroquois, Michel Thomas, and Nicol Taylor transported Peers's body on the next leg of the trip. It took them seven days to get from Fort Good Hope to Fort Norman (now Tulita). One night, on the seventh anniversary of Peers's death, the dogs began to bark. Over the barking, a man's voice was heard saying, "*Marché!*" Three days later, during another stopover, the men heard the same voice, over dogs barking, say, "*Marché!*"

When the four men finally made it to Fort Simpson, MacFarlane mentioned the voice to the chief trader of the district, Bernard Ross. The two determined that the voice was that of Peers, motivating the dog sled team to make it to Fort Simpson as quickly as possible.

✦

Media producer Andrew Silke, one of the founders of Paranorthern Encounters TV, has been investigating paranormal incidents in and around Yellowknife for a number of years. The company has been building an online community through its Facebook group. It's an attempt to gather stories from the territory and respectfully share them. Silke has found that while there are some who don't place much store in tales of hauntings and other paranormal events, there is a good deal of acceptance of them.

"[Yellowknife] is a very young city," Silke said, noting that while there are still stories of ghosts and uncanny events to be found, they're not easy to confirm.

The oldest buildings in Yellowknife are old cabins, but Silke hasn't come across any stories associated with them. "There's a kind of a ghost town near the Giant mine, but we don't have access to it because it's all being remediated by federal entities and you can't get in there without special permissions — it's just not safe."

Silke did point to some locations that have stories tied to them. Guests in the Explorer Hotel on 48th Avenue and the Quality Inn & Suites (formerly the Yellowknife Inn) on 49th Street have reported inexplicable occurrences. There have been reports from the third floor of the latter; bathroom sinks have turned on by themselves; guest have reported the feeling of someone sitting on the bed; and there have been sightings of an apparition of a man in old clothing and a miner's hat.

Another haunted location is a rehearsal space near Kam Lake. Musicians using the rehearsal space have reported seeing a young angry ghost. The stories have been shared in the *Haunted Canada* series by Joel A. Sutherland.[5]

Zhahti Kue, formerly Fort Providence, has a dark history. The Sacred Heart Residential School was located there. During the early 1990s, Albert Lafferty worked with the Mackenzie-Fort Smith Roman Catholic Diocese to use ground-penetrating radar near the site to determine whether bodies had been buried there. They uncovered a cemetery containing three hundred bodies, including 161 children. The only monument in Canada to honour the victims of the residential school system in Canada is located in Zhahti Kue.

Rankin Inlet, in Nunavut, has its own story of an allegedly haunted fire hall.[6] The spirit of a man, as well as the spirit of a girl by the ambulance bay, is said to inhabit the space, according to fire chief Mark Wyatt.

"A lot of these towns that have had dormitories and residential schools, there's either an energy around them that people are sensing, or it's a product of our environment," Silke said, admitting that most of the stories are anecdotal. "We get a mixed bag of stories that are speculation, and they're leads at the end of the day.

"They probably do have roots in the history, so ownership of those stories is vague," he added. "Is it an Indigenous story to tell, or is it just the facts?"

Both Silke and his brother are confessed skeptics, but what makes Andrew different, he admitted, is that he gets enjoyment out of trying to find explanations for the paranormal, while his brother is rooted in historical facts.

Some witnesses who share their stories with Silke, in particular Inuit, are very economical with their words.

"They're men of few words," he said. "So, it's hard to sometimes get details. People will just contact us, be like, 'This,' and we're like, 'What's up with that?' and they're like, 'I've seen it.'"

And of course, the conversation tends to go nowhere after that.

The hope for Silke is to compile stories and craft episodes of Paranorthern Encounters TV. But the focus will not just include the uncanny. Ghost towns are also a big part of the Northwest Territories. Pine Point was a mine on the southern shore of Great Slave Lake. It was an open-pit mine that was full of lead and zinc ore.

Now, the roads leading to the town are still visible from above, but the buildings are gone, moved elsewhere throughout the province.

Much like Pine Point, most of the buildings at Con Mine in Yellowknife are gone, but Giant Mine is still active and has less-than-savoury moments in history. On September 18, 1992, an underground explosion from a bomb killed nine miners: Chris Neill, Joe Pandev, Norm Hourie, David Vodnoski, Shane Riggs, Robert Rowsell, Malcolm Sawler, Arnold Russell, and Vern Fullowka. It was the denouement of a strike-lockout battle that was already heated.

Roger Warren was put on trial in September 1994, convicted of second-degree murder, and sentenced to life in prison.

"There's going to be other buildings in every city, in every town, it just comes down to knowing what your hotspots are and then drilling down from there," Silke said.

Nunavut

Nunavut is the most recent territory to enter Confederation. It was officially carved out of the Northwest Territories on April 1, 1999, thanks to work of Inuit leader and Chief Commissioner John Amagoalik. This was the result of decades of advocacy and negotiation.

In 1967 the federal government named Yellowknife the capital of the Northwest Territories. Inuit leaders in the eastern Arctic felt that this was too far away. So they began work to have a new territory created. In 1982 Tunngavik Federation of Nunavut was established to engage the federal government to deal with the outstanding land claims. By May 25, 1993, the Nunavut Land Claims Agreement was signed, and in June 1993, the Nunavut Act was approved by Parliament. Over those six years, the people of the proposed territory of Nunavut worked to establish government institutions. Iqaluit, on Baffin Island, was named capital.

Kenn Harper has lived in that territory for over fifty years — before it was even a separate territory. He's lived in Iqaluit, Pangnirtung, Qikiqtarjuaq, Padloping Island, and Arctic Bay on Baffin Island. And he also lived way up north in Qaanaaq, in northwestern Greenland. During that time, he has held various roles, including teacher, businessman, consultant, and municipal affairs officer. He's also known as a historian, writer, and linguist. He's also a member of the Royal Geographical Society and the Royal Canadian Geographical Society.

He also wrote a series of columns, called Taissumani, for the *Nunatsiaq News*. Taissumani means "long ago" or, more colloquially, "in those days." He was given free rein by the editors to write about anything, as long as it was anchored in history. "I wasn't teaching that whole time.... I was a vagabond for some years, just travelling around doing my thing, learning language and culture."

Nunavut has plenty of history, even though the modern territory is only a quarter of a century old. Humans have lived in the Arctic for thousands of years: the Inuit most recently and before them the Dorset and the Pre-Dorset. There have been plenty of bloody and macabre historical moments too. The most epic of those tales involves the HMS *Erebus* and HMS *Terror*. Both ships were part of the doomed Franklin expedition of 1845. The British had a long-standing obsession with finding a northwest passage so they could ship goods to and from Asia. Now, there are no ghostly hauntings associated with Captain Francis Crozier (*Terror*) and Commander James Fitzjames (*Erebus*); however, I imagine a lot of marine archaeologists lost a lot of sleep looking for the sunken vessels.

The wrecks of those ships were finally discovered on September 7, 2014, and September 3, 2016, respectively. Dan Simmons's book *The Terror* touched on their plight, taking the figures from history and dropping them into his own *danse macabre*. In true Stephen King–inspired fiction, there was a large hulking entity called the Tuunbaq that was controlled by a tongueless shaman.

Harper provided his thoughts on how pop culture misappropriates Indigenous beliefs, and he was not a big fan of Simmons's book.

"I've only skimmed the book ... but I know in the movie I saw, they refer to the spirit, ghost, the monster, whatever you want to call it, as *Tuunbaq*. Well, that's not even a word. That's a misspelling that made its way into the movie," he said.

The proper spelling is *tuurngaq*. What that is, is a spirit that has never been connected to a physical body. It can be a helping spirit as well as a vengeful spirit. Mostly they help angakkuq, who often aid in healing sickness.

Harper reminded me that there are regional variations for the names of deities. Sedna, in particular, is known by twenty different names from Greenland to Siberia and all points in between.[7]

"The North is pretty vast. A lot of people didn't talk about shamanism or old beliefs," Harper said. "They were afraid to talk about it, or didn't want to."

But there were legends shared, like Sedna, the mother of all sea mammals, that were designed to pass on knowledge to the next generation. Included in those legends were the taboos, or *pittailiniit*, the rules of life.

✦

There are more recent stories of unsettling events and spirt visitations in the territory. The vanishing village in the Kivalliq Region of Nunavut, located some 502 kilometres northwest of Churchill, Manitoba, as the crow flies is one example. John Robert Colombo wrote about the story in the *Halifax Herald* on November 29, 1930, which cited the source, correspondent Emmett E. Kelleher of The Pas, Manitoba.

Trapper Joe Labelle came upon the abandoned camp, with everything in its pristine form. The caribou-skin tents were still standing with belongings inside. Outside of the reported cairn, discovered by Labelle, there was nothing to explain his unsettled mind. "There was no sign of violence, no sign of trouble. The place was simply empty," Labelle said. He did, however, find two emaciated huskies. Kelleher reported that the RCMP was investigating.[8] Journalist Frank Edwards kept the legend going, writing about the village in his book *Stranger Than Science* in 1959.

More modern ghost stories involve the previously mentioned fire hall in Rankin Inlet. The firefighters there have had brushes with apparitions in their building. Firefighter Mark Kappi told APTN reporter Charlotte Morritt-Jacobs that he saw an older man and little girl standing on the steps of their fire hall.[9] "When I first saw it, I blinked my eyes and looked again. I opened the door, and he wasn't there no more," Kappi said.

Fire chief Mark Wyatt told APTN that he suspects it's the spirit of a former fire chief who took his life. Wyatt admitted that the young girl, however, could have been a victim of an accident and was transported in an ambulance.

Kappi admitted that he'd probably witness the apparition again. As for his commander, Wyatt, he had yet to see the alleged spirits, telling a reporter from *Up Here* magazine that the only thing he's witnessed is the constant issue of missing gloves.

"I've been here three years, I've spent a lot of time here, I've even made efforts to go out there and talk to them and see if they want to socialize or whatever," Wyatt said.[10]

✦

Those stories of spectral encounters and unexplained vanishings in Nunavut are more than just eerie tales; they are echoes of a deeper, long-standing tradition of supernatural beliefs that have endured for centuries in the North. From the mysterious vanishing village of the Kivalliq Region to the restless spirits of Rankin Inlet's fire hall, these tales speak to a connection between the living and the dead that remains unbroken by time.

Whether rooted in folklore, history, or personal experience, the persistence of ghost stories in Nunavut suggests that the unseen world still lingers at the edges of the everyday. As Inuit elders pass down legends and as modern witnesses add their own accounts to the growing lore, it becomes clear that the supernatural is woven into the very fabric of life in the North. The silence of the Arctic may seem vast, but if these stories are to be believed, it is rarely empty.

8

Ontario

Ontario has a lot of ghost stories. Like the rest of Canada, it has a history of human settlement that dates back over ten thousand years, and the Indigenous Peoples in the province have a treasure trove of stories and legends about the spirits that haunt the place — more on those in a later chapter. The Europeans, who arrived in the seventeenth century, have added to that lore. Long before the West and British Columbia saw the arrival of settlers, the newcomers in the province had begun telling stories of the uncanny. Another reason Ontario has so many ghost stories is because it has a lot of people. It is by far Canada's biggest province by population. According to Statistics Canada, as of July 2024, the population of Ontario was 16.1 million. Four of the country's biggest cities are located in the province. Toronto, the biggest city in the country and Canada's economic heart, has a population of almost three million. So, it's no wonder there are a lot of ghosts wandering about the place.

Cottage Country

Writer Andrew Hind has tapped into the history of Ontario from Cobalt to Muskoka to Niagara-on-the-Lake. His book *Ghosts of Niagara-on-the-Lake*

The Mather-Walls House in Keewatin, Ontario, stands as a testament to the milling industry in northern Ontario. Many people have reported hearing bangs, thumps, and footfalls in the house. But for one witness, the sound of the piano playing, and for another seeing a rocking chair move on its own, were enough for their blood to run cold.

(co-written by Maria Da Silva) highlights the history of the region, as well as its role in the War of 1812. In the book, he celebrates the region's ghost stories, but he casts a critical eye on tales he features too. He makes a point of separating the legends from historical fact.

Hind has always been interested in ghosts, having owned the illustrated book of Usborne Publishing's *World of the Unknown: Ghosts* as a kid, and reading *Fate Magazine* as a teen. While most kids grow out of their childhood interests, Andrew has continued to pursue the subject. He's found a lot of others who share his fascination.

"I think there is something universal in our thrill of being scared and in being curious about the afterlife," he wrote. "I'm not a paranormal investigator and am frankly skeptical by nature, but I find it all very interesting."

He's skeptical in part because of the difficulty of determining who saw what, where, when. Tales get told and retold and their connection to the truth of what actually occurred is quite often lost. Despite that, he believes that the retelling of ghost stories is important as it provides a way of preserving cultural identity and a nation's history entertainingly.

"I enjoy reading well-written and well-researched ghost books, so I guess as a writer, it was inevitable that I would try my hand at it myself," he admitted in an email. "Writing ghost stories uses different muscles as a writer than my normal work in travel, history, and lifestyle, which I enjoy."

Since most of Canada's ghost stories are rooted in our history, researching them for his books gives Hind a chance to dive into the history of a location and uncover stories and events that might otherwise go unnoticed. A fourteen-year-old girl told him she had read all of his ghost story books.

"That was a proud moment," he admitted. As a writer, he really values that kind of personal expression of appreciation. As a professional writer, he's happy that readers like his books enough to buy them. People like ghost stories, he acknowledges. "Ghost books sell well — which in itself says something about our cultural interest in ghosts — and that encourages publishers to ask me to write more."

One of the challenges Hind faces in writing his stories is actually finding a paper trail, something written that can verify a story, or at least part of it.

"Sometimes the legend doesn't match the history, and the legend wins, which is troubling from a historical point of view," he admits. He pointed to the example of Captain Colin Swayze at the Olde Angel Inn in Niagara-on-the-Lake.

As the story goes, in December 1813, the second year of the War of 1812, the "dashing" officer fell in love with the daughter of the owner of what was then called the Harmonious Coach House. Swayze was smitten by Euretta, and eventually she would reciprocate his feelings. He was so enamoured of her that when word got out of the American victory over the soldiers at nearby Fort George and the other British troops throughout the region made a hasty retreat, Swayze stayed behind.

He wanted to see Euretta one last time. And it cost him dearly. Learning of his presence at the inn, U.S. soldiers were sent to capture him. Swayze quickly hid in an ale barrel inside the inn. The Americans tore the place apart looking for the Red Coat. They used the bayonets on their muskets to stab the barrels. Finally, they found their mark. The young officer hiding inside the barrel was stabbed to death.

Euretta pushed her way through the throng of enemy soldiers and cradled her love in her lap one last time before he died. Not long after, the hauntings of the inn began. The ghost is seen predominantly in the basement — where the barrels were stored. It's a romance story fit for the movies.

Whenever I interview historians for articles, I often ask one question: "Is there a paper trail?"

In the instance of Swayze, Hind could not find a paper trail confirming his death in either the militia or the British regulars of Niagara. There's no confirmation that Swayze existed. But yet the story continues to persist. (The fact that "Swayze" is not just the supposed name of the ghost but also the name of an actor from a famous romance movie about a ghost makes it all the more likely that fiction has spilled over history.)

"What's important about the story is that for generations, it has reminded us of the fact that Niagara was occupied by Americans and that Americans were the enemy in the War of 1812," Hind added.

After writing at least a half-dozen books about ghosts from across the province, Hind did admit that when he first started, he was concerned about being seen as woo-woo. It's a negative term often used to describe anyone believing in the inexplicable.

"I suppose that motivated me to handle my ghost books in a professional manner, to separate my books from the plethora of ghost books written by enthusiastic ghost-hunting groups," he admitted. "I aimed to ensure my books were entertaining and well-researched, with the stories told accurately and authentically without sensationalism."

He not only wants to distance himself from the more sensational writers of ghost books, he wants to avoid being pigeonholed as someone who only focuses on one subject. Hind is keen on travel and history writing. He has written for publications like *Muskoka Life*, *Parry Sound Life*, *Toronto Star*, *Lakeland Boating*, *Horizons*, *Canada's History*, and more.

But somehow, he keeps coming back to the campfire tales.

"Ghosts have always been culturally significant as they are said to bring messages from the afterlife," Hind wrote. "The form ghosts take, therefore, can vary differently based on cultural norms and mores.

"Traditionally, ghosts and spirits have taken on very diverse roles and forms," he added. "In modern ghost stories, at least in the West, they tend to be lumped together and have lost much of their former specificity."

Hind has written eight books on paranormal happenings across the province, but his main focus is Cottage Country. But, one book, *Haunted Museums & Galleries of Ontario*, recounts the experience of a woman at the Whitchurch-Stouffville Museum.

The property, situated just east of Aurora, Ontario, sits along Woodbine Avenue. The Bogarttown School House (1857) was the first building, but more were added since 1971. The museum now includes the Vandorf Public School (1870), the Log Cabin (c. 1850), the James Brown farmhouse (c. 1860), a historic barn, and an outhouse.

The log cabin is said to have the ghostly presence of a woman attached to it. A woman named Vanessa who wished to withhold her last name told Hind about her experience and her attempts to communicate with the presence while she was visiting the centre in October 2015. She heard the raspy voice of a woman and asked for the entity to make itself known. Vanessa grew cold and then took out her phone to snap some photographs.

Streaking white lines were on several of the images. Was it paranormal? Vanessa admitted that she thought so.

"People are not afraid to share stories, at least not in my experience," Hind wrote me. "Many of them are professionals who have nothing to gain, aren't craving attention, and likely would have much to lose in terms of reputation if they were to be ridiculed."

But they share, regardless, whether it's a farmer out on the Saskatchewan prairies as per Catherwood, or the Lord Mayor of Niagara-on-the-Lake at a book signing with Hind.

"I would have thought an elected official would have been reluctant," Hind admitted of Patrick Darte. "He was anything but."

In fact, he has found very little hesitation in his investigations. Most people are happy to share their stories. It seems that other writers have had success digging up stories too because Ontario has no shortage of ghost story books. John Robert Colombo has written a glut of books during his career. Mark Leslie Lefebvre has written specifically about Hamilton, Ottawa, and Sudbury.

Ottawa

Before we mosey into Ontario's largest city, let's talk about a few little stops along the way. Some iconic haunts in the province need to be shared.

No. 1 would be Ottawa's first jail and quite possibly the creepiest ruins in Canada. A close runner-up would be Hamilton's Hermitage. They're iconic because of their tie-ins with history.

The old Carleton County Gaol, now a youth hostel, sits in the middle of Ottawa's downtown core, just a stone's throw away from Parliament Hill. Built in 1862, it was quite possibly one of the most inhospitable places in the country. Many innocent people were sent to the jail, including those suffering from mental health issues.

What happened at the old (Not Ritz) Carleton was the kind of stuff that made Agnes MacPhail, the first woman elected to Canada's House of Commons, lobby for prison reforms in the country. In *Haunted Ontario Revisited*, Terry Boyle describes the terrible conditions in the jail. Inmates were not allowed to shower; they were hidden away from sunlight and fed the bare minimum.[1] Women, children, and men were all jammed into the jail. Once boys hit the age of twelve, they were moved in with the general male population. The screams of women and children are often heard by those spending the night, and by staff.[2]

On the fourth floor of the prison, a faceless woman in what appears to be a blanket has been seen, and in the secret staircase that connects what was the governor's house to the prison reads an inscription that was uncovered during restorations in 1972: "I am a non-veridical Vampire who will vanquish you all. One by one I will ornate your odorous flesh with famished fangs. But Who? Are there 94 or 95 steps to the 9th floor? A book on the top shelf will lead you on the right path."[3]

The vampire ghost is said to have caused the warden's eight-year-old son much distress. He became sick when the family moved into the governor's quarters, and his personality shifted.

Disembodied screams, a faceless woman in a blanket on the fourth floor, and a vampire ghost skulking about in a secret staircase are not the most interesting things to be found in the jail, though.

Canada is known as a relatively peaceful nation, so it should come as no surprise that the list of politicians assassinated in the country is low. In fact, only two people have been assassinated in the entire time our country has existed. The first was Thomas D'Arcy McGee, whose assassin, Patrick Whelan, was housed and eventually hanged in the Carleton Jail. (Pierre LaPorte, the other politician murdered, was killed by his kidnappers during the October Crisis of 1970.)

Whelan was a sympathizer of the Fenians, a group of Irish ex-pats who wanted to hold Canada for ransom in exchange for the independence of Ireland from England. He was hanged on February 11, 1869, before a crowd of over five thousand people.

Now, according to Terry Boyle, superstition typically dictated when prisoners were hanged back in those days. If the normal practice had been followed, Whelan would have been hanged on the thirteenth day of the month. If that was not possible, they would be hanged at the thirteenth hour of the day. The noose would also have thirteen coils.

Whelan was on death row for ten months, which was an unusually long time. While he was on death row, he became friends with his prison guard, John Lyle. The guard came to believe that Whelan was not guilty, that he was just a convenient scapegoat.

Whelan's hanging ended up taking place on the eleventh hour of the eleventh day of the month. He was buried with the noose around his neck, and his wishes to be buried in his family's plot back in Montreal were not honoured. Perhaps because normal practices weren't followed when Whelan was executed and because his wishes weren't honoured when he was buried, his ghost still haunts his prison cell in the jail.

From a political capital to an industrial capital, The Hermitage, just outside of Hamilton, is another familiar haunt that is merely a shell of its former self. The mansion, located off Sulphur Springs Road, is located on a property that has been home to a string of bad-luck stories. The first involved Reverend George Sheed, who purchased the land and built a humble home on the property. He was building his first church on Mineral Springs Road, but he died before he could see it finished.

Then, a former English colonel, Otto Ives, purchased the land in 1833. He settled there with his wife and his niece. A servant of Ives, William Black, fell in love with the niece. When he asked Ives for the niece's hand in marriage, the elder blew up and said no servant was going to marry his niece. Black, seeing no more reason to remain alive, hanged himself from the branch of a tree. Ives, knowing the lad could not be buried in consecrated ground because of the suicide, buried him at a crossroads.

Mark Leslie notes in his book *Haunted Hamilton* that the crossroads would become known as Lover's Lane. It is said Black returns to hang from the tree he hanged himself from on nights of the full moon.

The next owners of the property, the Leith family, built a stately manor on the grounds in 1855. George Brown Leith's youngest child, Alma Dick-Lauder, would live in the stately mansion until a fire claimed it in 1934. After the fire, she had a smaller home built on the property, and Dick-Lauder lived there until 1942 when, at the age of seventy-nine, she finally shuffled off this mortal coil.

It seems, though, that she's never really left. Even though her mortal remains were interred at St. John's Anglican Church in Ancaster, she still haunts the house. It's said an engineer interested in studying the mansion ruins once saw her watching him from afar.

Dick-Lauder was very dedicated to preserving family history, so perhaps she keeps watch over her family's ruins.

Toronto

It must be said that Toronto has not done a great job preserving the city's heritage. I've learned to appreciate this city. I've lived here for over fifteen years. I grew up just outside the city, where there is a deep-seated disdain for anyone living in Toronto. I almost feel like Benedict Arnold for moving here, but I've learned to live with it.

After all, Benedict Arnold had his reasons for being a turncoat.

The thing is, Toronto is an interesting place. It's one of those cities that seems to be rapidly destroying its past. It seems that it can never say no to the developers determined to raze the city's architectural legacy in favour of new condos. When it does occasionally manage to stand up to the forces of "development," more often than not the province overrules the city, allowing "construction" companies to continue destroying our past. The buildings that do get heritage status these days appear to have questionable value, except as proxies for the buildings the city didn't protect from the wrecking ball.

But enough axe grinding. In between the glass-and-concrete condos going up, there remain a few little pockets of history. These are reminders that Toronto has a past, whether developers and politicians want to acknowledge it or not.

In those landmarks walk ghosts.

One of those is J.P. Rademüller, who haunts the Gibraltar Point Lighthouse. On the side of the lighthouse, completed in 1808, there's a plaque from the Ontario Archaeological and Historic Sites Board acknowledging the alleged haunting. It reads: "The lighthouse, one of the earliest on the Great Lakes, was completed in 1808. The hexagonal tower stood fifty-two feet tall and was topped by a wooden cage that enclosed a whale-oil lantern. The mysterious disappearance of its first keeper, J.P. Rademüller, in 1815 and the subsequent discovery nearby of part of a human skeleton enhanced its reputation as a haunted building."

Rademüller sailed across the Atlantic and settled first in Nova Scotia. He had worked for King George III and the British Royal Family. He eventually found his way to Canada. He quickly fell in love with the burgeoning nation and eventually found his way to York (Toronto's original name). He netted a job as the first lightkeeper of the lighthouse and then, boom, war broke out.

With the War of 1812 in full swing, Rademüller's job was suddenly even more important. He had to keep the British fleet safe from the shoals of the harbour. One lost ship in the harbour could have spelled doom for the British. On January 2, 1815, before any peace armistice was signed, he was murdered. The suspects were two soldiers from the Gibraltar Point blockhouse on the island located across the harbour from the city. The two, John Henry and John Blowman, who were visiting Rademüller at the lighthouse, had had too much to drink, and Rademüller cut them off. The two men were not happy and chased him up the lighthouse stairs, where he was inevitably pushed off the top.

Knowing that the punishment for murder was death, they allegedly hacked up his body and buried it in different spots around the lighthouse property.

There is little printed material about the murder, Adam Bunch writes in *The Toronto Book of the Dead*. He notes that a former lighthouse keeper, George Durnan, shared the story, but he considered it to be more of a fairy tale than a factual account of the happenings.[4]

Maybe Bunch is a bit too skeptical. He says there's no evidence of a trial, but in his book *Haunted Toronto*, John Robert Colombo says there was one on March 31, 1815. According to him, the two men were acquitted. Colombo cites Diane Beasley, a historian from the Marine Museum, and Michael Moir, an archivist from the Toronto Harbour Commission. Both agree that the story has been embellished over time, and both note people have reported that on cold nights a ghostly keeper can be seen in the area.

✦

The stories of Rademüller and other restless spirits have been investigated and chronicled by a number of groups and individuals over the years. One of the earliest websites was Obiwan's UFO-Free Paranormal Page, which was launched by Las Vegas resident Elizabeth Busch in 1994. It had content dating to 2021 but has since vanished. The Toronto Ghosts and Hauntings Research Society (TGHRS) was one of the most important organizations investigating haunts and compiling stories. The TGHRS website was launched in October 1997. Following that, the Ontario-based ParaResearchers was born in April 1999 after they investigated Ghost Road on Scugog Island. Finally, a national website, Paranormal Studies and Investigations Canada (PSICAN), launched in spring 2005, was established. It covers everything within the realm of paranormal: cryptids, UFOs, and ghosts.

"The [T]GHRS was one of the first groups to have an online presence in Canada," Sue Demeter, one of the co-founders, wrote me in an email. "There were other, much earlier ghost groups, but it was one of the very first with a website and discussion boards in North America."

An important paranormal investigator is Michelle McKay, who has been carving her own path throughout the streets of Toronto for a number of decades now. She grew up in a haunted house in East York, and her curiosity in an afterlife began at the tender age of ten.

"My grandmother used to have the priest come in and do exorcisms on the home," she admitted during a June 2024 phone interview. "So, I ended up going to the library at ten years old and started doing research on the paranormal."

From the occult books she found tucked in the back of the basement of the library, she learned some of the techniques that she has used over the years in her paranormal investigations. She experimented with EVPs, automatic writing, and other evidence collecting. When her friends caught wind of what she was doing, they started inviting her over to their homes to check for ghosts. "It just never stopped," she admitted. "Next thing you know, I'm in the newspapers."

McKay's grandmother and mother both discouraged her from investigating any further, partially because McKay's distant cousin was Esther Cox. Yes, the Esther Cox of Amherst Mystery fame.[5] Additionally, her great-uncle, Henry McKay, was the first director of MUFON Canada (Mutual UFO Network Canada). So, there's a long tradition of studying paranormal activity in her family.

Eventually she would learn about her uncle's work, and he would try to get McKay to investigate UFOs too. "One of the things he taught me about UFOs," Michelle says, "is that even though UFOs are unidentified flying objects, you can't assume they're aliens. 'We don't know really what they are. They could be something interdimensional; they could be from another planet.' I looked at him and said, 'Yeah, it could be a ghost.' He kind of chuckled and said they could be ghosts."

McKay started Coldspot Paranormal Research in Toronto in 2002. With over two decades of investigating paranormal activity, she has an understanding of how Canadians respond to the paranormal. "I've never had an issue with getting them to talk to me. Once they know I'm a paranormal investigator, then they tend to talk," McKay said, adding Coldspot.org has grown into a huge database of ghost stories. She's been collecting stories through the website since its inception.

But businesses aren't quite as open to investigating — or drawing attention to — hauntings. There's always a concern that somehow they'll be impacted negatively if it's believed that their premises are haunted.

"When I investigate businesses, I'm kind of on the lookout for that," McKay said. "Now these big corporations have bought the bigger hotels, and there's a lot of red tape to hop through."

McKay doesn't really understand why companies and organizations avoid the paranormal, even when the location is widely known as being a cold spot. Some companies have told her that they'd be willing to allow her to conduct an investigation, but only on the condition that it be kept private.

"I don't do that anymore," she admitted. "I used to do cases where it was completely private. I would agree not to go public with it at the beginning when I started paranormal investigations.

"If I go to a location and I find evidence of the paranormal, then I couldn't tell anybody about it. If I caught an apparition on film or if I caught voices on an audio recorder that I thought was good evidence, I couldn't let anyone listen to it." She no longer is willing to keep her discoveries private. "If I can't bring it to the public to say, 'Look what I found,' what's the point?"

While she's hardcore when it comes to businesses and organizations, she's more understanding of individuals. If someone in a private residence requires assistance, she will provide her services. She practises the utmost discretion. But it still presents the same challenge.

✦

Ontario has a rich trove of lurid tales, scary stories that are fun to share around the campfires. There are haunted locations all over the province, from small towns like Baden, just west of Kitchener, and Cobalt, just north of North Bay, to the big cities of Toronto, Hamilton, and Ottawa. The urban stories are often bigger and bolder, linked to such things as assassination plots, mass hangings, and angry quarrels after the booze gets put away.

Because of province's relatively long colonial history and its larger population, the province has more ghost stories than the rest of the country. It seems that Ontarians are happy to share those stories; they love to talk about ghosts. Toronto, which likes to think of itself as "Toronto the Good," has a dark past, as can be seen in stories like Rademüller's, and more and more, its citizens are interested in discovering the stories about that past.

9

Quebec

Ghost stories have been associated with Quebec since before European exploration of North America, as the Mohawk First Nation Kahnawá:ke has called the land home for a thousand years. They have their universe of ghost stories and oral traditions that pre-date Jacques Cartier's voyage up the St. Lawrence River on June 9, 1534.

The influence of the Roman Catholic Church was felt back in 1608 when Quebec City was founded. Then, as settlements cropped up along the St. Lawrence River, so did the Catholic Church's teachings, right up to when Montreal was founded on May 17, 1642.

"When the British took over, they brought their own ghost stories," history buff Donovan King said. "Especially the Irish and the Scottish."

Montreal

"When the French arrived here, they were kind of religious zealots," King said. He runs the Haunted Montreal tours, leading those interested in chilling experiences on ghost walks, paranormal investigations, and haunted pub crawls.

King has travelled a lot throughout the United States and many other cities, but the one thing he couldn't understand was why fifty different companies were trying to "cut each other's throats. Everyone might have their different way of telling a story, but I'm not into this idea of holding it close to my chest," he told me. "I want it out there."

So, he wrote blogs detailing the history of Montreal from the Irish Famine Cemetery in Pointe–Saint-Charles to the Hôtel Place d'Armes and all points in between. Montreal is brimming with history, or what King refers to as its eras.

According to the Irish embassy, ninety thousand Irish immigrants landed in Quebec in 1847. The theme of newcomers does factor into the Haunted Montreal tours. There's also that element of activism on King's tours. He calls out the harsh realities of colonialism and scientific experiments that exploited the vulnerable. So much history has transpired in Montreal that there are bound to be people who have survived the darker aspects of the city. "Historically, they have been used to cover taboo topics," he added. "In the Victorian era, they could cover venereal diseases, homosexuality, prostitution, all this taboo stuff. And to this day, they still can — we can talk about Indigenous, resistance, and genocide."

It's a great way to get to the truth, for King. Even though the stories border on fiction, they challenge the binaries of reality and the paranormal.

"It's not just like regular storytelling. There's this really weird realm where you're telling a story that's both real and paranormal, and yet neither real nor paranormal in a sense that zombies are both alive and dead," he said. "It creates this ontological realm that's very disturbing to people. That's why people love these stories so much."

King is accommodating and sensitive to other cultures. He would love to share some of the Mohawk oral traditions like the Kanontsistóntie — a cannibalistic spirit that drove inhabitants of New York away from their homes — on the Haunted Montreal blog but does so only if they are approved by the elders.

"I'm not going to appropriate them in any way unless I have permission and collaboration," he said, adding he has worked with paranormal groups in and around Montreal like Dominique Desormeaux and Entre deux tombes (Between Two Tombs) to flush out more stories and lore.

Of course, there are still lots of stories to tell, and King has found there is real interest in the stories he shares. He says that there is an openness in Montreal to discussing the paranormal. "This is largely a francophone culture, and it's rooted in that colonial project, which was superstitious like crazy," King said. "They love these legends. There are books and books of these types of legends."

When it comes to the smaller English population in the city, King mentions that parts of the Haunted Montreal tours are geared to the culture of pub crawls. They do one every week in English, but only once a month in French.

"Pub crawls aren't part of the French tradition, and we're trying to make it so because it's a huge tradition in England, Ireland, and Scotland," King said, with a laugh. "That's what you do. You go on a pub crawl."

The most famous story in Montreal, in King's eyes, is the story of Marie-Joseph Angélique, a Black slave who attempted to escape her bondage. She was accused of starting a fire that led to the Merchants' Quarter being razed in 1734. No evidence was provided, yet she was convicted, tortured, and hanged. She was forced to walk down the street in a white gown, called a chemise, with a sign around her neck stating her crime: *Incendiaire*. She carried a torch to her execution site, which was on the grounds of the burned Merchants' Quarter.

She was burned on a funeral pyre, and her ashes were spread along the road. It is said that her spirit has been seen walking along Rue St. Paul in Vieux Montreal.

"Through this ghost story, you can reveal the horrors of slavery," King said. "You can reveal the horrors of this 'medieval justice system.' You can really shed light on this New France society through this type of story."

The famous tale of "The Willow Bunch Giant," Édouard Beaupré, shows how ghost stories can shed light on darkness.

Beaupré was an exceptionally tall man, reportedly eight foot two. When he was young, he wanted to be a horseman but unfortunately, he grew too large to ride a horse. He eventually became part of a travelling freak show.

He died on July 3, 1904, while in St. Louis, Missouri. Instead of sending his body home to his family, his remains were preserved and placed on display in the Eden Musée in Montreal and then moved to the University of Montreal's Faculty of Medicine.

"Eventually, he looked like Frankenstein's [monster]. He was all cut up and sewn," King said. "Finally, someone had the good sense to say, 'Okay, enough's enough. We're sending him home to Saskatchewan.'"

While his body may have at long last found its way back to a proper resting place, it is said that his spirit still bangs on pipes in the basement of the Monument-National on St. Laurent Boulevard.

The tale of Simon McTavish is on lighter side. He was a rich eccentric — he made his money being a fur trader and the founder of the North West Company, the Hudson's Bay Company's competition. A rich man, he decided he needed a grand house and so built a Scottish castle in the baronial style high up on Mount Royal. But perhaps his privilege led to his undoing.

McTavish would often walk from Old Montreal to see his home being built on Mount Royal. One night, he was caught in a rainstorm. He got a cold, and it became pneumonia, which became pleurisy, and the next thing you know, he's dead.

His castle was never completed, and it sat exposed to the elements. Parts of the castle would be used to construct the Duggan House on the McGill University campus, which itself has many ghostly tales. McTavish's long-since abandoned castle was demolished in 1861, and the rubble — what wasn't used in the construction of the Duggan House — was piled onto his mausoleum. Students who were part of the snowshoeing club would scamper up Mount Royal and raid the old man's tomb. Not long after those exploits, people began to report seeing McTavish tobogganing down the hill in his own coffin.

Naturally, that scared Montrealers. There wasn't really much to be scared of, though. King admitted that the tobogganing ghost was just a prank. "Resurrectionist" students who were climbing the hill in winter to rob paupers' graves in the Catholic Cemetery would ride them back down the hill to the campus on toboggans.[1]

"We've done a lot of work to revive the Simon McTavish story, because it was very much unknown," King admitted. "I decided to delve into it, and

I couldn't believe the complexity of the story ... They just tried to erase the story, and that's largely because they wanted to convert the mountain into a park."

The university has lots of ghostly tales, but there are quite a few other parts of the city that are home to wandering spirits. A lot of the early stories revolve around Griffintown, which was a landing spot for a lot of Irish immigrants who came to Montreal during the nineteenth century.

It is here, in this small village of shanties, that Montreal's Mary Gallagher comes to life. She was a working girl in the Griff. She was thirty-eight and never had any problems finding clients, according to Mark Leslie.[2]

"According to the Haunted Griffintown ghost walk's account of her story, the events that would lead to Mary Gallagher's demise began rather pleasantly on June 24, 1879. She had gone out with her friend and fellow prostitute, Susan Kennedy, to celebrate Saint-Jean-Baptiste Day, a holiday in Quebec. The town was filled with music and festivities. It was fun; it was also perfect for picking up johns," Leslie and Krishnasamy wrote in their book as a lead-in to when stuff got real.

The story of Gallagher's death is fit for a Hercule Poirot tale, as no one quite knows who did the deed. Both Gallagher and Kennedy picked up a man, Michael Flanagan. He was smitten with Gallagher and they went off together. Shortly after, her body was found but her head was missing.

Amazingly, it was not Flanagan but Susan Kennedy who was considered suspect No. 1. This might have been the result of bias — Kennedy's profession made her suspect in the eyes of the law. As well, Kennedy was also not liked by her neighbours. In the end, she was tried and found guilty. The judge sentenced Kennedy to hang on December 5 that same year.

Kennedy never did hang, though. Prime Minister Sir John A. Macdonald commuted her sentence to a prison term. She served sixteen years in Kingston Penitentiary.[3]

Sounds like a straightforward true crime story. The reason it's considered a ghost story is simple. Every seven years since Mary's death, she makes her way to the corner of William and Murray Streets looking for her head. So, that means the next time we see her will be June 27, 2026. Don't lose your head over it, though, because Mary's ghost hasn't been seen since the 1920s.

The Grey Nuns Residence by Concordia University in Montreal has some creepy history appended to its timeline. It's home to Concordia University students during the school year and has served as a hospital and an orphanage. It is said to be haunted by the ghosts of orphans who died in a fire on Valentine's Day in 1918.

✦

While there's a lot of interest in the stories King shares via his tours and blog, there are definitely some in Montreal who are not so happy to have him talk about ghosts. For example, King's stories about the Grey Nuns Residence on the campus of Concordia University resulted in him receiving some pressure from the institution's legal team.

The Grey Nuns, or les Sœurs Grises de Montréal, are a Roman Catholic order founded in 1737 by Marguerite d'Youville and a small group of other women. First called the Sisters of Charity Montreal, they dedicated themselves to caring for the poor, sick, and abandoned in Montreal. They took over the Hôpital général de Montréal in 1747 and established hospitals, schools and social services across Canada.

The Grey Nuns Motherhouse, built in 1871, serves as a student residence for Concordia University. In the basement, there's a crypt where 276 people are buried, including the remains of 232 Grey Nuns who resided in the motherhouse.

It is widely believed that the building is haunted. Some of the students report strange noises and sensations. Some believe these things are caused by ghosts of the nuns who are buried there. There are many children buried there also, some the victims of a fire that occurred in the building in 1918.

But not everyone in the city, or the province, wants to hear lurid tales about the Grey Nuns being entombed in a student residence, especially the college administrators.

"When we first started that tour, I got a call from Concordia lawyers, and they said, 'We don't want you talking about the nuns.' And I said, 'Well, why not?' And they said they might be offended," King recalled.

Most of the Grey Nuns who are still alive are in their nineties, and King, tongue-in-cheek, said they aren't online. It took some negotiating and he had to play around with the narrative a bit, but in the end, he was able to share their story on his blog.

Universities aren't the only organizations that wish to avoid being linked to the paranormal. Like almost everywhere in Canada, it seems that the hotels in Montreal aren't all that keen on advertising the fact that they may be haunted.

So at what point does a corporation or hotel want to embrace its paranormal lore?

"It could bring in a lot of business," King admitted, adding that when he stayed in Savannah, Georgia, they billed the city as the most haunted in America.

To borrow a phrase that's part of our modern parlance, America goes over the top when it comes to the paranormal.

"It's a different approach down in the States where they're like, let's exploit this. Whereas up here, there's a huge reluctance in many cases, but once they do embrace it, they do it really well," King said.

He tours other cities, gauging how dark tourism is presented so he can come back to Montreal and work on building relationships with businesses, like the Queen Elizabeth Hotel, to best present the grim and macabre.

Regardless of corporate hesitancy, King admitted that Montreal respects its paranormal history. "It's really fascinating to just pick one story and to delve into the historical background behind it," King told me. "That's what I tend to do on my blog. Honestly, my blog's almost at a hundred, and I've got another four hundred [topics] on the list and I get new ones every month."

And people keep showing up for his tours. "It seems that there's an awful lot of people interested in it, engaging in it, again from all levels of society, Indigenous, French, and English, and new immigrants as well," he said. "I'm often surprised at how many people I get on my tours from places like China or India because they have their own universes of ghost stories."

✦

There is so much more to Quebec than its largest city. Travel north to the Quebec side of the Ottawa River, and you will find Shawville, home to one of Canada's first-ever poltergeist cases: the Dagg Poltergeist.

In 1889 George and Susan Dagg adopted an eleven-year-old Scottish orphan, Dinah Burden McLean. Soon after, mysterious events began occurring. CBC broadcaster and historian Richard S. Lambert would write about the incident in his book *Exploring the Supernatural*. It was reported that starting September 15 of that year and continuing past November 17, spontaneous fires were lit, stones were thrown by invisible hands, and articles like water jugs were thrown about the house. Plus, an entity was seen by the children in the shed out behind the house. They saw it in different forms, including a tall thin man with a cow's head, horns, and cloven feet; a big black dog; and a man with a beautiful face, long white hair, and dressed in white.

Aventure Outaouais includes the Dagg Poltergeist location on its haunted tour of Pontiac County every October. I spoke with Brandon Bolduc in 2022 for a Superstitious Times article. "They got all the notables in the town, the priest, the mayor, come witness, and they all signed a document that is still in the archives in Shawville," Bolduc told me back in October 2022, adding that the girl was mistreated by her adopted parents. "The Dagg haunting is one of the most famous hauntings in western Quebec."[4]

The *Ottawa Citizen* covered the story on the 125th anniversary of the exorcism that rid the spirit for good from the community.

Playwright Greg Graham wrote a stage play and it was performed in 2010. He told the newspaper that if it had been performed in the United States it would have had more of a following.

"There would be a small, thriving industry around this story if we were in the U.S.," Graham says. "Maybe there will be yet?"[5]

The entity left, supposedly at the behest of journalist Percy Woodcock, who witnessed some of the events and wrote about them in the *Brockville Recorder & Times*. His efforts were aided by members of the community who sang hymns. However, when modern-day journalist Chris Lackner found the original farmhouse and spoke to current residents Charlene and Derec Lombard, it appears there's still a presence there.

"We would hear stuff running in the ceiling, and it's like, well, is it a squirrel? It doesn't sound like a squirrel. Is it a mouse? No. It doesn't sound like a mouse. If it was a mouse, it would be the mouse Olympics," Derec Lombard told Lackner during the video segment.

Some posited that it was a hoax, and others believe there could be psychokinesis involved, but 125 years have passed and sometimes, instead of a case of broken telephone, the lines are simply dead.

✦

No province wants to be left out of the forlorn bride trope, so we'll share Quebec's tale of a femme fatale jilted at the altar. Just outside of Quebec City you'll find the Montmorency River and Montmorency Falls. La légende de la Dame blanche is a tale that takes the romance of waterfalls and gives it a Stephen King twist.

As the story goes, the year was 1759 and Mathilde Robin was courted by true love, Louis Tessier. He was a farmer and a member of the militia. He asked for her hand in marriage and Mathilde's dad granted permission. The wedding was set for the end of the summer.

However, the Seven Years' War was being fought at the time — this war between England and France was fought in North America as well and resulted in the British forces defeating the French forces in Quebec and taking control of the province (and other French territories in North America). Tessier was called into action to fight. He never made it to see Mathilde again.

In the days before the war, when Tessier was still alive, Mathilde would meet her love at the Montmorency Falls. Following his death, she donned her wedding dress, walked up the falls, and threw herself off from the top of the falls. It's said that people can hear her mournful cries as she forever searches for her Louis.

Quebec City

Cantiane Breton works with Ghost Tours of Québec. She's been with the team for ten years at their base of operations in Vieux Quebec, not far from the Citadel. Naturally, the focus of the tours is its spooky history. There's a lot of history, which isn't surprising given the wars, diseases, epidemics, murders, and executions that took place in Quebec. Throughout her time as a guide, she's experienced some strange activity, like shadows, silhouettes, noises, and footsteps.

Breton has talked a lot with her colleagues about ghosts and what they mean to the Québécois. "We came to the same conclusion … people don't usually talk about ghosts. When we go around to different institutions to ask them if we can use their stories in our tours, they usually say no. They don't want to be associated with that and they don't see that as a good publicity."

She used the example of hotels not wanting to share their ghostly lore because they don't want to advertise that someone died there. In Quebec City, the Château Frontenac stands atop Cape Diamond. Louis de Buade de Frontenac, who the hotel is named after, is said to still hang around. His presence was felt during the hotel's renovations in 1993.[6]

Breton said she doesn't suspect that people's unwillingness to talk is related to a fear of ghosts. "Usually, when people fear a ghost, it's because they think they are relatives or people who might be in their houses — it's more personal to them," she said. "On the tours, though, people will come and talk to us about ghosts. We're outside or in other places and because we're in those settings, people are more likely to open up."

One of the stories that people like to hear about is the legend of la Corriveau. In season 2, episode 1 of *Creepy Canada*, host Terry Boyle addressed the cultural importance of la Corriveau throughout Quebec and Canada. "Occasionally, a ghost story goes beyond being a tale and becomes an integral part of local culture," he said. "In Quebec City, the story of la Corriveau is just that. A woman found guilty of witchcraft and murder has become a beloved part of Quebec history."

Marie-Josephte Corriveau, who lived in Lévis, was on her second marriage. When her husband, Louis Dodier, was found dead, rumours began swirling that she was involved in his death. His body was found in his barn, and after an initial postmortem, it was thought he was kicked in the head by a horse.

As a result of the rumours, the British army decided to investigate Dodier's death. They brought Corriveau and her father, Joseph, before a military tribunal of twelve English officers on April 15, 1763. The first trial found her father guilty; however, he claimed that he was merely an accessory. A second trial was conducted, and Corriveau ended up admitting her guilt, allegedly adding that she killed her husband because of the way he treated her.

She was sentenced to hang on the Buttes-à-Nepveu in April 1763, near the Plains of Abraham. Her body was taken down and placed in an iron gibbet, which was hung at the crossroads of what is now Rue Saint-Joseph and Rue de l'Entente in Lévis until May 25.

She came to be seen as a martyr, a Québécois woman killed by the British army. Her story became widely known, and almost immediately supernatural elements were added to it. Her ghost, it was claimed, accosted passersby at the crossroads where her body was hung. Further embellishments came over time from writers like Philippe Aubert de Gaspé, Louis Fréchette, Sir James MacPherson Le Moine, and William Kirby.

"Not so long ago we were quite heavily Catholics," Breton admitted. "We had this whole link with hell and death and the population was ruled by this fear of death and this fear of the devil."

Many of the folk tales of Montreal involved the devil, especially "La Chasse-galerie" ("The Flying Canoe"), which featured lumberjacks making a deal with the devil on New Year's Eve so they could be back home with their sweethearts. They flew back home in their canoe but were instructed to stay away from churches.

"This fear is still there," she admitted. "People believe that it's not something they should talk about. It's something that they try to avoid as much as we can because it's associated with the devil and so is quite scary."

Obviously, not everyone is scared, because tourists and residents of Quebec City descend on Vieux Quebec and take part in the walks. Breton noted that some of the people travelling to Quebec City have tried to go on all of the ghost tours across the country. There's a deep interest in history of all kinds, not just the history of the rich and powerful, she believes. Ghost tours allow us to peer into those experiencing disenfranchisement and poverty.

The interaction with people on tours was what Breton enjoyed most when she was a guide on the tour. It was her way of testing the crowd, to find out who was skeptical and who was open-minded.

But sometimes, trying to find source material about the uncanny is enough to make you question your curiosity. When researching, Breton mentioned that it is difficult to find the general history of Quebec and Montreal.

"There is a lot of information about Montreal, but Quebec ... we have a few books that gloss over a few topics," she said, adding her colleagues really have to dig for details. One colleague has referred to herself as a "rat and she just digs until she finds what she needs to find."

✦

As ghost stories and folklore continue to be passed down, they shape the cultural identity of Quebec in ways that are both subtle and profound. Whether rooted in history or legend, these tales reflect the fears, beliefs, and imaginations of the people who tell them. For Breton and her fellow guides, these stories offer more than just entertainment — they provide a way of keeping history alive, ensuring that the voices of the past, whether spectral or not, are never truly forgotten.

10

Atlantic Canada

European settlement in what would one day become Canada began in Atlantic Canada and Quebec. We started this book in the West. British Columbia was a relatively old colony compared to the Prairies and the North, but as you move to the East, you move back in time — at least in terms of European settlement.

The settlers brought with them Old World myths and legends that slowly evaporated as younger people emigrated to other parts of Canada. They were part of the Great Migration, and waves of them pushed through into the Maritimes.

Nova Scotia

If you've ever been to a kitchen party after a wedding or visited older relatives in the Maritimes, you're bound to hear a few stories of strange happenings and magical beings. And after a few drinks, they'll begin to tell you stories that will counter the warm feeling in your belly.

And that's what sets the Maritimes apart from the rest of Canada. It may be, because the Maritimes was the first part of the country to be settled by colonialists, that its folklore keeps alive older stories and myths than the other, more recently settled parts of the country. And because, more than any other part of the country — apart from Quebec — most of its inhabitants can trace their roots in the region back centuries, that old lore lives on.

Life was hard in those early times, and death struck the inhabitants down earlier and in harsher ways. The Maritimes, simply put, is a region where people are fully aware of their mortality, and it has manifested in their stories. The stones of the Fortress of Louisbourg were used to build homes in the community, thus spreading the energy from the traumas experienced there to other residences. The phantom ships on the waters of Chaleur Bay and the Northumberland Strait are reminders of the disaster that can strike sailors and others who venture out onto the seas.

From New Brunswick to Newfoundland, Maritimers are more in tune with their folklore, and it resonates more deeply with them. The stories of spirits are more than just fodder for campfire tales. There is a belief in the preternatural.

The Maritimes seem to be the epicentre of shareable paranormal phenomena in Canada. And over the years, many of those stories have been collected into books. Retired RCMP officer Elliott Van Dusen, a paranormal investigator who has hosted a couple of paranormal symposia in Halifax, attributes the birth of his interest in all things paranormal to the work of folklorist Helen Creighton, who wrote the book *Bluenose Ghosts* in 1957. It would be republished in 2009.

"She started out by going around and collecting all the folklore from all the older people because, you know, once they die, you lose that oral tradition," Van Dusen said. "She went out and collected a bunch of stories. She was your first paranormal author or investigator."

Van Dusen's love of lore also extends to his career in law enforcement. *Supernatural Encounters: True Paranormal Accounts from Law Enforcement* and *More Supernatural Encounters from Law Enforcement* were collections gathered from first responders.

"Some of the people that would tell me their ghost stories, they would tell me flat out 'I don't believe in ghosts, but all I can tell you is what I saw and what I experienced,'" Van Dusen recalled. "Then they tell me the story and, in my mind, Yeah, no doubt that you just saw like a ghost.

Former RCMP officer and Paranormal Phenomena Research & Investigation founder Elliott Van Dusen goes for a ride with a haunted monkey doll that he acquired from a Missouri man. The relic was part of the young man's uncle's estate. It would be found in different parts of the house, forcing the man and his girlfriend to lock it in a trunk. Van Dusen collects allegedly haunted or cursed items.

"Even they have trouble kind of like admitting that it was something that they couldn't explain."

Even though there is hesitance, the East Coast does not shy away from a good tale, especially when it relates to mariner lore.

"Nova Scotia's a great province to be a paranormal investigator in because there is a lot of interest in ghost stories, folklore," he told me during a December 2023 Zoom conversation. "At the Paranormal Symposium we held, there was a lot of interest in more of the newer stuff."

"Nova Scotia is loaded with folklore because of our Scottish, Irish, and English history," Van Dusen said. "It's obviously one of the older parts of Canada, and they still have beliefs in northern Cape Breton — they believe in fairies, which is an Irish belief."

Van Dusen has never had to investigate anything about fairies; however, it remains a pervasive belief throughout the Maritimes, in Newfoundland in particular.

Still, it's a topic that comes up in literature about the Maritimes, especially in Colombo's book *Ghost Stories of Canada*. The first story in the book introduces us to the fairy folk "who hold hands with the host of Angelic Beings and find favour in the eyes of sensitive men and women, kindred spirits of the New Age in the New World."[1]

Little people were always discussed in the old country. You had redcaps and leprechauns in Ireland and the fae in Scotland, and those traditions carried over into Newfoundland, Nova Scotia, New Brunswick, and Prince Edward Island.

Folklorist Barbara Rieti is Canada's foremost expert in all things fae and wrote about the wee creatures in *Strange Terrain*.

> It was March 1940. It was raining hard that night. Now I had no oil clothes or nothing, but still I was as dry as I am right now sitting here at this table. I left Mt. Carmel four o'clock in the evening and never reached home until one o'clock in the morning. I came to Colinet and travelled across the ice to John's Pond. I was on my way home from John's Pond to North Harbour and it was at the Beaver Pond that the fairies attacked me and took control of the horse. Whatever way I'd turn her, she'd head back toward John's Pond. The fairies would not let the horse leave the pond. So I tied the horse to a stump of a tree on the side of the pond. And you should hear the gibberish and singing all around me. It nearly sent me batty. No man would believe the singing, dancing, and music of these fairy characters. They were so handy they were within reach. When the cloud left, I put my head close to the water, and I saw little things on the side of the bank, around eighteen inches high, like rabbits. I tried to catch them, but they played all around me. They were teasing me. So I said, "Have your

> way, ye damn things." I left them alone and went back and lay on the sled. I was going to stay there the night. I stayed for so long and couldn't stand it any more. No prayer was any good. So I made oaths and swore on them. It was just like an orphanage when I started swearing. Such crying and screeching you could hear as the little creatures left and went eastward. The horse's eyes lit up the pond. When I finally got home, I untackled the mare from the sled and instead of going to the barn she headed right back up the hill again. I was from four o'clock to six o'clock in the rain, but still me cravat didn't have a speck of rain. After that the horse couldn't be held going across the pond. Others wouldn't ride her at all on the pond because she travelled so fast. Once she got off the pond, she was back to her own pace again.[2]

It's fascinating that there's considerable interest in fairies on the East Coast, not to mention some real belief in them. Although fairies are not popular among the paranormal investigators, people still do explore the phenomenon. Van Dusen is more interested in other paranormal happenings, however. One that really intrigues him is the Fortress of Louisbourg.

The fortress was built from 1713 to 1740 by the French, who used stones imported from abroad to Cape Breton. The first British siege of the fort took place in 1745. A second siege occurred in 1758. That siege was one of the battles the Seven Years' War, which ended with the defeat of the French at the Battle of the Plains of Abraham.

Cape Breton paranormal group Haunts from the Cape has investigated the historic landmark and uncovered uncanny phenomena in the fortress's buildings, including the King's bakery, the Duhaget house, the military chapel, and the de Gannes house. It was in the de Gannes's house that a camera captured a strange figure robed in a fur shawl.

Employees and investigators alike have also reported eerie experiences in other areas of the fortress. The postern tunnel beneath the Dauphin demi-bastion has been the site of spectral sightings, while the Duhaget house stands out — one employee even felt an unseen force hold them back from tumbling down the stairs. With its history of conflict and upheaval, it's no surprise that Fortress Louisbourg is considered one of the most haunted locations in Nova Scotia.

Without a doubt, the most famous ghost story in the Maritimes is the Great Amherst Mystery. As mentioned earlier, the happening centred on Esther Cox and her experiences with a poltergeist.

In the fall of 1878, Esther Cox shared a house with her younger sister, Jennie, their brother, another sister, Nelly, the eldest sister, Olive Teed and her husband, Daniel, as well as their two children. The haunting of Esther Cox began with unexplained knocking sounds echoing through the Teed household in Amherst, Nova Scotia. Soon, objects were thrown across rooms, furniture moved on its own, and Esther suffered violent seizures, fevers, and swelling. The disturbances escalated when messages appeared on the walls, including the chilling phrase, "Esther Cox, you are mine to kill." Witnesses, including doctors and townspeople, reported seeing objects levitate and fires spontaneously ignite. The activity lasted for fifteen months, drawing widespread attention and ultimately inspiring Walter Hubbell's book *The Great Amherst Mystery*, which spread the legend far beyond Canada's borders.

Despite the sensational nature of the events, some skeptics, including Laurie Glenn Norris and Barbara Thompson in *Haunted Girl: Esther Cox and the Great Amherst Mystery*, have suggested alternative explanations for Esther Cox's experiences. They argue that her troubled upbringing, marked by instability and trauma, may have contributed to the alleged poltergeist activity. Additionally, Walter Hubbell, who initially sought to debunk the claims, later speculated that the disturbances began after an assault by Bob MacNeill, adding a psychological dimension to the mystery. The presence of spiritualism in the Teed household, including séances and mesmerism, further complicates the narrative, leaving room for both believers and skeptics to interpret the Great Amherst Mystery in different ways.[3]

Every year, there's a festival in Amherst, Nova Scotia, close to the New Brunswick border, where they pay homage to Esther Cox and the ordeal she went through.

"Another story that's received a lot of attention is the Fire Spook of Caledonia Mills," Van Dusen said. "I know there were books written about it."

The home of Alexander and Janet MacDonald, located in Caledonia Mills — a predominantly Scottish community about twenty-three kilometres southeast of Antigonish — was plagued by poltergeist activity from 1899 to 1922. Strange lights, peculiar noises, mysterious fires, and unexplained movements of animals and household items tormented the family, which included their adopted daughter, Mary Ellen.

In 1922 the MacDonald farm became the centre of a chilling series of events known as the "Fire Spook." The family experienced unexplained phenomena, including spontaneous fires — thirty-eight ignited in a single night — furniture moving on its own, and livestock being freed or mysteriously relocated within the barn. These disturbances gained widespread attention, prompting an investigation by Walter Franklin Prince of the American Society for Psychical Research. Prince concluded that Mary Ellen, then about fifteen years old, was acting as a medium for poltergeist activity, possibly in a dissociated state, suggesting she might have been unaware of her actions.

The MacDonalds eventually abandoned their home, and the haunting has since become a well-known part of Nova Scotia's folklore.

A tale that has survived the test of time and is quite emblematic of the Maritimes is the story of the Lady in Blue who walks the shorelines of Peggy's Cove. A young woman named Margaret is said to be waiting for her love. The origin of the cove's name isn't known for sure; it's believed by some that Peggy's Cove gets its name from the wraith that awaits her love. Just as there is some dispute about the origin of Peggy's Cove's name, there are different camps concerning the identity of the ghost. Some maintain that she is not, in fact, a forlorn bride; rather, they argue that Margaret was the lone survivor of a shipwreck, and she was searching for her children who were on board the ship with her.

"Occasionally the Lady in Blue appears aware of the living and actually tries to speak to a tourist who's come to admire the view. Any who have had this experience say that they haven't been able to understand what she was trying to say, that it seemed as if the grieving mother's word were swept away by a gust of wind. The people who've shared such an encounter all say that she seems to be reaching out across time, imploring them to help her."[4]

The history of the Maritimes is full of shipwrecks, and it's no wonder that more than a few ghosts have been linked to those. One of the greatest tragedies in Canadian history occurred in Nova Scotia on December 6, 1917. Two ships collided in the Halifax harbour; one was a fully loaded munitions ship bound for the front lines of the First World War. The explosion was the biggest one caused by humans before the introduction of the atomic bomb in 1945.

According to the *Canadian Encyclopedia*, almost two thousand people died, another nine thousand were injured or blinded, and another twenty-five thousand were left homeless.

This catastrophic loss of life left many ghosts wandering the area surrounding the harbour, and there are quite a few haunted locations associated with the explosion. One of the most popular seafood restaurants, the 5 Fishermen, on Argyle Street, is one of those locations.

It was originally built in 1817, and at the time of the explosion, it housed Snow and Sons Mortuary. Some of the victims of the *Titanic* were brought there when that ship sunk in 1912, and it was also where bodies recovered from the 1917 explosion were brought.

"Some folks will tell you that the current kitchen was once the processing room for the cadavers; however, I haven't been able to find a floor plan of the original mortuary to verify such a claim," author Steve Vernon wrote in *Halifax Haunts: Exploring the City's Spookiest Spaces*.[5]

New Brunswick

Macro-tragedies can have a profound effect on the community, but even micro-tragedies can have an impact. Travel west from Nova Scotia to New Brunswick, and you'll come across the Dorchester Jail. The original institution, which is now a bed and breakfast, was built in 1875, and the building remained a functioning jail right up until 1998.

It is alleged that twenty-seven men are buried there. "The graves are all unmarked, so we don't know where exactly they are, but they're back there somewhere," co-owner Natasha Marsh said to me during an August 2023 interview for the Superstitious Times. "We don't mow the grass where we think they are because we don't want to bother, disrespect, or disrupt anybody. I've got to live here with them, so we play nicely."[6]

Marsh has witnessed several apparitions in the section of the former prison she calls the Dark Side. It's there where prisoners on death row would be imprisoned. They would await their date with the noose and witness those before them fall through the trap door.

Two brothers, Arthur and Daniel Bannister, were hanged together. They were seventeen and twenty, respectively, and they were hanged for killing Bertha and Philip Lake and their son, Jackie, during a botched kidnapping. It's widely believed that the two were innocent, that they were the fall guys for their mother's crimes.

Their mother, May, wanted them to kidnap the Lake's five-month-old daughter, Betty Ann, so she could blackmail her parents. The two boys did it, with some help from their sister, Frances, but she was not charged.

The Algonquin Resort in Saint Andrews, New Brunswick, has a laundry list of ghosts affixed to it, including a night watchman, a bellhop, a crying bride, and a little boy named Ben who fell out of a window chasing after his ball.

It is suspected that their spirits are among those still inhabiting the former prison. Their presence no doubt adds to the fun of anyone spending the night at the bed and breakfast.

Skip north and you'll come across another spooky sight. Ghost ships are a trope in Maritime tales. Chaleur Bay in Bathurst, New Brunswick, and the Northumberland Strait both are said to have phantom ships that appear to those on the coast.

Chaleur Bay's ghost ship is typically in the Bathurst Harbour, and it glows as if it were afire, while people along Seacow Head in the Northumberland Strait watch a three-masted schooner sail into the shoals during squalls. Those sightings have been happening since 1786.

Prince Edward Island

"Captain Angus Brown of Wood Islands recalled that he and his crew had taken the ferry *Prince Nova* out from Wood Islands at night to bring aid to a ship that appeared to be burning. As they approached, it vanished,"[7] Julie V. Watson wrote in the second edition of her book *Ghost Stories and Legends of Prince Edward Island.*

The stories of phantom ships, forlorn women searching for their children claimed by the sea, and tales of sea serpents are everywhere in the lore of the Maritimes. Although the stories of the spirits are inevitably sad, they also offer comfort. In telling these tales, Maritimers remember the dead. They offer a way to connect and heal from those traumatic experiences.

Not all the stories of hauntings are directly related to the sea, although inevitably some kind of link can often be found. The Yeo House in Tyne Valley, west of Summerside, is the former home of James Yeo Jr., a shipbuilding magnate who reaped the rewards of being on the north shore of the island. Today, the building houses the Prince Edward Island Museum and Heritage Foundation. Matthew McRae, executive director of the museum, told me that staff have experienced weird goings-on inside the walls of the 1860s building.[8]

An old toy was discovered in the walls of the house. Dubbed "Wheelie," the toy was placed in one spot when the staff closed up the museum, but then the next morning, Wheelie was found somewhere else.

The house also has an overwhelming male presence lording over the property. Some suspect it is James Yeo Jr. keeping an eye on his home. Other people have reported hearing female voices and screaming.

McRae left me with one key quote that I think is great to repeat here as it's the Maritimes in a nutshell:

> P.E.I. has got a huge tradition of folklore and storytelling, and it's very strong even now in the province. I think partly that's because of this strong sense of community and provincial identity that keeps these stories alive that might not be as alive in a larger community where there's a lot more movement and action.
>
> These stories kind of stick around and become a part of the family and even community traditions, and I think that Wheelie is a reflection of that.

Newfoundland

If you like history and folklore and have a penchant for the eerie, follow Dale Jarvis on social media. His Haunted Hike posts on LinkedIn are like a blast of fresh Atlantic air. Jarvis is the executive director of the Heritage Foundation of Newfoundland and Labrador, which won a Governor General's History Award for Excellence in Community Programming.

Jarvis started the Haunted Hike in St. John's in 1997, and he has been a fixture for those interested in all things folkloric and paranormal since then. Unfortunately, the twenty-fifth anniversary of the Haunted Hike fell during Covid-19, so the troupe was unable to celebrate. "It felt like a reminder: 'Oh, time is meaningless,'" he joked.

But time and its passage are important to Jarvis. He feels a duty to keep the history of Newfoundland alive and to celebrate some of the province's more well-known hauntings like the Bell Island Hag and those in the LSPU Hall, Newman Wine Vaults, and Christian's Pub.

The Bell Island Hag is the tale of a young woman who was walking along the coastline. She happened to witness German U-Boats being restocked, and the men rushed her. She was dragged to a nearby swamp, where she met her end. She had cried out for help, but superstition kept the locals from coming to her rescue. According to Barbara Smith in *Great Canadian Ghost Stories*, Nathaniel Hammond had a run-in with the Hag that left him deeply shaken. Some report hearing her cries to this day.

The LSPU Hall, one of the most haunted buildings on St. John's Victoria Street, sits on land with a long and storied past. Originally home to the First Congregational Church of Newfoundland, the site has been home to multiple buildings, many of which were destroyed by fire. A building known as the Temperance Hall was built on the site following the Great Fire of 1892; in 1912 the Longshoremen's Protective Union (LSPU) purchased it. Today, it is a thriving arts centre.

The hall is known for eerie activity, including apparitions, shadowy figures, and phantom footsteps. Its most famous ghost is Fred Gamberg, a beloved fixture of the St. John's music and arts scene who drowned in 1995. Since his passing, his spectral presence has been reported in the theatre, watching performances or lingering in the wings — perhaps unwilling to leave the place he loved.

Nestled in the heart of St. John's, the Newman Wine Vaults stand as a testament to the province's mercantile past and its deep-rooted ghostly lore. The Newmans, originally fish merchants in the sixteenth and seventeenth centuries, expanded into the port wine trade, taking advantage of Newfoundland's cool climate to refine their product. According to legend, a storm-battered ship sought shelter in St. John's in 1679, leading to the accidental discovery that aging port in the region enhanced its flavour.

The vaults themselves, with their sturdy stone and red brick construction, date back to the early nineteenth century and have served a variety of purposes over the years, from storing wine and tobacco to holding everyday goods like potatoes and bleach. But beyond their commercial significance, the vaults have acquired a spectral reputation. Since the site's restoration in the late 1990s as an event space, reports of unexplained sounds, phantom knocks, and fleeting shadows have fueled speculation that the spirits of the past still linger, making the vaults a chilling intersection of history and hauntings. Remember to say hello to Steve if you should happen to visit the event space.[9]

Another ghost you should say hello to is Maggie over at the Christian's Pub on St. John's famous George Street. The city's oldest watering hole, a famous spot for "screeching in" visitors, has a resident spirit that messes around with equipment behind the bar and makes a racket on the second floor. Maggie — no one knows if that's her real name — has been seen on the main floor sitting in one of the church pews wearing a long white dress. It's suspected that she came with the pews that were once inside the Congregationalist Church on Queen's Road.

The oldest ghost story is connected to the UNESCO World Heritage Site, L'Anse aux Meadows, which dates back to 990 to 1050 CE. The Vikings were here, and the story of Leif Eriksson is told in the *Saga of the Greenlanders* and the *Saga of Erik the Red.*

The haunted tale relates not to Leif but to Thorstein Eriksson. He went to Vinland (Newfoundland) to recover the corpse of his brother, who had been shot with a Skraeling[10] arrow. On the voyage across the Atlantic, disease broke out and Thorstein died. His wife, Gudrid, who was also on the ship, mourned her husband's death.

As his body was laid out on the ship, he sat upright asking for his wife. He asked three times, but his wife was too afraid to respond. One of the crew, also named Thorstein, asked the spirit what he wanted. He gave Gudrid a prophecy of her life after his death.[11]

"That is the oldest ghost story that is told about what may or may not have been Newfoundland," Jarvis said, chuckling. "After that, it gets vague for eight hundred years or so."

That's not the only Norse tale, as there are many reports in L'Anse aux Meadows about the sounds of boats coming to shore in the night, and of people talking in a foreign language that isn't English or French. But yet, no one came to shore.

There's also a famous mermaid account from 1610, but we'll save that for another book. But from the mists of the coast came the story of the Island of Demons. And it appeared on maps.

"It was known as a haunted place, and there are all kinds of legends that then came out later and were popularized in the 1800s and 1900s," he said. "There was a tradition of quasi-supernatural things that were happening here very early."

One related story related is that of Marguerite de la Rocque, who travelled with her uncle Jean-François to the New World. Marguerite had her servant, Damienne, with her. Enroute, she fell in love with a young man on the ship named Étienne Gosselin.

Marguerite's uncle wasn't happy with the relationship. Jean-François waited until the ship was near the haunted Isle of Demons and then sent his niece, her servant, and Étienne to the island, giving them only a small store of supplies. The trio did their best to survive. They foraged for food, eating animals they were able to hunt and using the pelts to try to protect themselves from the bitter Atlantic winds. Things became even more difficult when Marguerite became pregnant. Before she gave birth to her son, Étienne and her servant had died; the infant only survived a few weeks. The grieving mother managed to survive when she flagged down a passing fishing boat. The crew eventually took her back to her family.

There is no Isle of Demons off the coast of Newfoundland, but many suspect the island in question to be Harrington Harbour, which is part of Quebec.[12] There's even a landmark there called Marguerite's Cave.

By the early nineteenth century, there was an explosion of supernatural tales in the province. During the Victorian era, everyone was obsessed with ghost stories, and the lore of Newfoundland was shared far and wide.

"Starting late in the 1800s and early 1900s, you start seeing the beginnings of folklore collection in Newfoundland," Jarvis said. "*The Journal of American Folklore* was filled with Newfoundland ghost stories and supernatural stories."

Like the other Maritime provinces, Newfoundland is littered with shipwreck stories. Tales of phantom ships are also very common. And one trope is the predictive nature of ghost ships. If one sees a ghostly vessel, it's assumed that the ship went down in the same kind of weather that the person who witnesses the ghost ship is experiencing.

"That kind of weather lore, which may or may not have a ghost in it, is seen as something that's made up or legendary. It's part of a natural process," Jarvis said.

There many be an actual historical account of the ship going down, but over time, the actual story of the shipwreck morphs into a ghost story. "These stories function as a sort of memorialization. It's something that distinguishes it, so it becomes a more tellable story," he said. "It's a way of perpetuating oral history. The ghost story makes it more interesting but has the benefit of keeping the historical event alive."

Out-of-the-way locations also have a whole load of lore. Take, for example, Bell Island. The tales of the island became more widely known when the Beyond the Haunting Investigations team investigated both the #2 Mine on Bell Island as well as the Bell Island Hag of Dobbin's Garden for their series *History's Most Haunted*.

Bell Island has a fascinating history of iron ore mining. The island's mines operated between 1891 and 1966. There were a total of 106 fatalities during that time. One accident, in 1938, killed two men and injured seven. A methane gas explosion occurred in the #6 mine.[13] The spirits of some of the dead miners are said to still haunt the tunnels.

The Bell Island Swamp Hag is the rather mean name given to the spirit of a young woman who stumbled upon the Nazis when they tried to invade the island during the Second World War. Supposedly, she was dragged into the swamp and killed. Residents did not come to her aid either because they feared the Germans or because they were fearful of the fairies that are said to be common on the island.

"It's definitely a place that has accumulated a lot of stories over the years," Jarvis said. "It's just generally a weird spot. I think part of it might be that Bell Island ... was a spot where everyone came to work in the mines — came from all over around the bay — so then there was a greater concentration of stories coming from different places.

"It was a bit more of a melting pot," he added. "That might be one of the reasons why there are more supernatural stories for Bell Island than there would be in similarly sized communities, because all these people suddenly came when the mine opened and brought their stories with them."

✦

So, what do Newfoundlanders think of the paranormal now?

No one thinks you're weird if you tell ghost stories in Newfoundland. "The modern Western view of things is that there is a division between natural and supernatural," Jarvis said. In Newfoundland, it's not always so clear that something is natural or supernatural."

Premonitions, or strange visions, are called tokens in Newfoundland. "[People] might see a figure of someone at the time of their death or just before they die," Jarvis admitted to me during the interview. "Those things aren't necessarily seen as being supernatural. Those things are just part of the natural worldview."

The appearance of a token, for further reference, may also be precognitive.

"Many things have been interpreted as signs, omens, or tokens of a coming death. These have included strange rapping noises on the side of a house or the sudden stoppage of a clock," Jarvis wrote in *Haunted Shores*.[14]

11

Indigenous Spiritual Knowledge

There is no paranormal. The spirit world is just part of our world.

It just is.

I first spoke with spirit investigator Erin Goodpipe by phone for the Superstitious Times in October 2021. I had just finished writing a lengthy feature about the lack of diversity in the paranormal community and had sought out Indigenous sources. With only one source tracked, I wrote the feature. A few weeks later, I fortuitously connected with both Goodpipe and Mi'kmaq Paranormal's Tee Sock for separate articles and later returned to them to talk about the impact of both residential schools and the Sixties Scoop on Indigenous spiritual beliefs for a *Haunted Magazine* article.[1]

That's the reason I spoke with Goodpipe again about this book. She's incredibly knowledgeable about social-political issues and is in tune with the spirit world. The thirty-six-year-old is Dakȟóta and Anishinaabe and has appeared on APTN's *The Other Side* and T+E's *Paranormal Revenge*.

I spoke with her via Zoom in October 2023, hoping to get a little more perspective on the spiritual beliefs of Indigenous people. Keep in mind, according to the Government of Canada, there are over 630 First Nations communities in Canada. They represent more than fifty nations and fifty

Indigenous languages.[2] And they have been living here since long before the Europeans decided to show up like unwanted guests. Archaeologists like Jacques Cinq-Mars estimate the Bluefish Caves in the Yukon Territory had inhabitants living in them twenty-four thousand years ago.[3]

I wanted to know more about Indigenous beliefs on spirits and the afterlife. Though I was not sitting with Goodpipe in person, she has a responsibility not to share very specific details about Dakȟóta and Anishinaabe culture with non-Indigenous people. Goodpipe is quick to acknowledge that she doesn't speak for all of those communities.

"We have a lot of diversity as far as our protocols, our beliefs, and our understandings," she said. "There are so many nations across what we call Turtle Island."

It's important to Goodpipe to remain humble, and not to be seen as an expert in all Indigenous knowledge systems.

"I have been having more and more conversations with people who are working in the field. It's part of the decolonization work," she added.

She's quick to point out that the paranormal is "really white." It's something I've addressed in an editorial in the past.[4] With so many different people in the world, and so many different beliefs about what happens after we die, why is that only a few white paranormal investigators and writers control the narrative?

"If you're writing a book about the paranormal in Canada, you have to talk about that history and the different cultures that are here, specifically, Indigenous people who have been here for thousands of years," Goodpipe told me.

For Goodpipe, her Indigenous beliefs are rooted in the belief that we are spiritual beings who for a time live on Earth. But there is a spirit realm around us.

"Everything in creation has imbued spirit or spirit value," she shared. "And because of that, we live relationally. We're always trying to honour our relationship with other parts of creation."

There is an afterlife, and our existence on Earth should be spent always trying to become better people and live righteously by a code of ethics. "We understand that when we move on, we also receive a judgment," she said.

Ancestors play a major role in ceremonies and understandings, and although it is often very fragmented, communication does happen with them. "That's hard to explain in English, but there's a communication that can happen for only a specific amount of time," Goodpipe added, saying her grandfather would talk about death often.

Death is a topic that white Canadians typically avoid. But there is a normalcy to it in the stories shared by Indigenous people.

✦

Canadian and Ojibway scholar Basil Johnston has written many stories involving the manitou. The manitou is the spiritual life force behind everything, from the environment to organisms to events in Ojibway beliefs. In their creation story, Kitchi-Manitou, or Great Mystery, creates Turtle Island, creates the world, plants, birds, animals, fish, and the other manitous "in the fulfillment of a vision."

The world was flooded. The skies were changing, and the animals clung to the surface, watching as Geezhigo-Quae (Sky Woman) changed. The animals then asked a giant turtle to offer his back for a place of rest for Geezhigo-Quae. As she lay on the back of the turtle, she asked for soil. The only animal able to fetch soil was the muskrat. Geezhigo-Quae used the soil to trim the rim of the turtle's back. She then breathed life into the soil. Then Geezhigo-Quae gave birth to twins, whose descendants would be the Anishinaubaeg. Other nations would arise from them, such as the Ojibway, Ottawa, Pottawatomi, Algonquin, and Mississauga.

The island continued to grow and became a continent, the Land of the Great Turtle, and Geezhigo-Quae granted ownership and stewardship of the land to the people in joint tenancy with the manitous, birds, animals, insects, and generations yet to be born.

It became Johnston's goal, as he shared in the preface of his book *The Manitou: The Spiritual World of the Ojibway*, to share the stories of the manitou.

> Stories about the manitous allow native people to understand their cultural and spiritual heritage and enable them

> to see the worth and relevance of their ideas, institutions, perceptions and values. Once they see the worth and relevance of their heritage, they may be inspired to restore it in their lives. Perhaps other people will find worth in our understandings as well.[5]

In my interview with Goodpipe for *Haunted*, she echoed Johnston's words. Goodpipe told me that those who ran residential schools for the government admonished Indigenous people for believing in the supernatural, or pantheistic deities. Religious leaders at the schools used physical and mental abuse to force Indigenous children to abandon their beliefs and adopt Christianity.

"Their goal was to steal the Indian out of the child," Goodpipe told me. "Their goal was to assimilate the Indigenous into the body politic."

According to Goodpipe, the stories that have been recovered and shared mean everything to Indigenous people. "They explain why we're here. They explain how to live a good life, the ethics we must follow to live in harmony with one another. We're people of stories — and those stories are sacred," she said. "We tell those stories at certain times to honour and teach how we're supposed to live spiritually."

So, the spiritual world — a spiritual life — is important to Indigenous people. Now, when it comes to investigating ghosts and spirits, Goodpipe sees it as an everyday thing. "Indigenous people are always researching and investigating the spirit. We have to because it's a part of our identity," she shared. "When you go back, and you become a part of a ceremony, you're learning about Indigenous knowledge and you're trying to apply that, become it — you are always addressing that spiritual component."

Paranormal investigation builds on that spiritual relationship, but the formal investigations also include tools of the trade. In today's parapsychological studies as well as spirit investigation, the goal is to look for evidence, not proof.

Most investigations use tools like electromagnetic field detectors and digital recorders to capture electronic voice phenomena.

"I'm always really cautious of who I work with, what their intentions are," she admitted. "I truly believe when you call upon spirits, you're opening doors, and it can be dangerous. My people understand that, and you can see that in the way that we conduct ceremonies," Goodpipe added. "It's not like we have ceremonies all of the time. We're not talking to our ancestors all the time and we can't all do it. No, there are very sophisticated understandings about how to do it and what tools to do it with."

Those who have the gift of being spiritual mediators are trained to perform ceremonies, and that training takes years and years. The ceremonies are hard, both for those conducting them and for those in attendance.

In part, parapsychological studies involve the study of the survival of the body after it dies. It makes no difference who is investigating in the field. Indigenous beliefs offer another way of considering the spirit journey after someone dies.

"For each nation, there are specific details around what that looks like," Goodpipe said. "I was very fortunate that I'm involved in my traditions. I have a community where we can go back and do what's culturally safe and right for us to help that spirit move on and for us to process and mourn here on Earth in a healthy way."

The ceremonies allow relatives to talk with the dearly departed before they move on. And they're not short. They are long and involve specific steps. Goodpipe admitted that performing these ceremonies can be burdensome in a way, but it is a fulfilling process. It offers a way of honouring those who have died.

If she works with someone on an investigation, they have to know the proper procedures. She says you can't just jump into an investigation with physical tools. The use of intuitive gifts like mediumship, retrocognition, clairsentience, as well as hypnosis, among others, can be dangerous.

During her work on *The Other Side* TV series, Goodpipe would address the audience and stress that what they're seeing is being performed by investigators who have done it for a long time, and that they have spent days performing ceremonies to prepare for the investigation.

"You often just see the actual investigation, but there's a lot of prep work that actually goes into that investigation," she said. "My investigatory work involves really understanding people's intentions and their tools and spending an appropriate amount of time evaluating the situation and evaluating if I'm in a good place to do something."

Oftentimes, Goodpipe won't open doors unless there's an elder or someone who's qualified to hold spiritual space for what she and her team are about to do. She also won't do an investigation without medicines.

According to Mi'kmaq psychic medium Shawn Leonard, "The Medicine Wheel represents all of creation and our connectedness with all people and elements of our world."

The four medicines are included in that. The North, the white quadrant of the wheel, uses sweetgrass. The East, the yellow quadrant, uses tobacco. The South, the red quadrant, uses cedar. And the West, the black quadrant, uses sage.[6]

"In my investigatory work, I strive to stay true to my indigeneity. I make sure that I'm challenging the paranormal investigative world that wants to just get some entertainment, that's just interested in telling a spooky story or shock value — getting screams and scares."

The goal of Goodpipe is to show the world that there is a spirit world. When she mentioned that in our discussion, it reminded me of how resistant Canadians and Americans are to talking about death — not entertaining stories about death or lurid true-crime stories of murders but real, personal experiences with death. It contrasts so clearly with the attitude of Mexicans, with their celebrations like *Día de los Muertos* and the observance of *Santa Muerte* as a protective entity and psychopomp.

"It's interesting," Goodpipe admitted. "I feel like it would change investigations if we, as investigators, or our people, had an understanding of death and life. It wouldn't be so spooky. That's part of the fear factor. It's this uncertainty of whether people are gone and dead.

"In Western culture, there's these endless investigations of tragic death. It's trauma porn," she said. "We're using other people's stories to garner a response that is about entertainment. But again, if people had an understanding about death, then maybe it wouldn't be so shocking."

Goodpipe was a subject matter expert on the series *Paranormal Revenge*, which blended true crime with the element of the paranormal, though she didn't choose the stories that she commented on.

Although the narratives revolved around trauma and revenge, she always looked to humanize the characters, not demonize them. "I think it's important when considering a spirit to recognize that this was a human being. The question is, 'How do we empathize with them even when what they're doing is horrible? How can we understand why they're doing it?'" she asked.

As part of the investigation, she believes it's necessary to get into the headspace of the spirit causing the havoc. To try to understand them but not to justify the behaviour.

A show like *Paranormal Revenge* did push the envelope for Goodpipe. She admitted it broke a cardinal rule for her. Episode 1, "Love You to Death/ Photo Negatives," involved a tale of spousal abuse. "Since I was not there in person, it wasn't possible to get a full understanding of what was going on. It's really hard to conclusively say, 'This is happening because of this,'" she said. "With spousal abuse, I never want people to watch this and start blaming spirits. I don't want people to say, 'Let's stay in a relationship because it could be a spiritual thing.' I think the better thing to say is 'No, you should probably leave.'"

The relationship between real-life trauma and the spiritual life of the Indigenous Peoples in Canada is something that comes up again and again in our discussion. The impact — physical and mental and spiritual — on the Indigenous children sent to residential schools has been touched on. The effects of that and the Sixties Scoop on Indigenous spirituality are still being felt.

"One of the smart things — smart in a really bad way — the Canadian government did was to try to break the bond between Indigenous children and their families and communities. They saw the connection between our older people and our younger people, whether that's grandparents, grandchildren, or parents and their children, aunties, uncles; they saw that there's something really powerful about that connectedness for our people," she said.

Initially, the government insisted that Indigenous children attend day schools; they could go home at the end of the school day. However, the government changed the policy and insisted that the children go to residential schools, boarding schools, when they realized that Indigenous cultural traditions were still being passed down. "Because they wanted to civilize us, they tried to kill the Indian in the child," Goodpipe said. "They knew they needed to separate young people from the rest of the community, and that's because knowledge is transmitted experientially, orally from old to young. If you strip children from having that access, then they're not going to get that knowledge."

So, the children and grandchildren were taken away from their families and placed into the residential school system, severing the intergenerational passing of spiritual knowledge. The government-created residential schools existed from the 1870s to the 1990s. The Mohawk Institute in Brantford, Ontario, was the first church-run residential school, opening in 1831. The last one was Kivalliq Hall in Rankin Inlet, which closed in 1997.[7]

The Sixties Scoop is the term given to the mass removal of Indigenous children from their families and subsequent placement into the child welfare system. This occurred without the consent of their families or bands. The federal government began phasing out compulsory residential school education in the 1950s. Instead of sending children to residential schools, the government abducted them and gave them up to be raised by white families. By the 1970s, one-third of children in foster care were Indigenous.[8]

"The Sixties Scoop and residential schools were forced upon our people; the government was bent on destroying those relationships," Goodpipe said. The spiritual knowledge of the Indigenous Peoples in Canada became fragmented, as those who taught oral traditions were forced to go underground. Government agents were appointed to reserves to ensure Indigenous practices were not being practised.

Goodpipe, who is from Saskatoon, Saskatchewan, was adopted into her spiritual family through a *hunka* ceremony and has been able to learn the knowledge and traditions that others were deprived of. She admitted in our *Haunted Magazine* interview that she was "fortunate enough to be in a space of privilege."[9] The ceremonies and knowledge she has learned have been vital when investigating the spirit realm in Canada and the United States.

Growing Up Spiritual

Travel to the East Coast and you'll meet Mi'kmaq Paranormal co-founder, Tee Sock. She's had a deep interest in the paranormal for quite a while, but it wasn't until 2016 that she formed her investigation team with friends Sheri Bernard and Julie Pellissier-Lush.

The paranormal isn't something that's talked about in Mi'kmaq culture. It's something they grow up with. "It was quite normal for us as children to sit with elders and hear their version of what experiences they went through," she recalled during a phone conversation. "It could have been taking a walk through the woods and this happened."

They talk about all kinds of things: whether or not the Devil exists; the importance of never closing your door on the hungry or homeless. Sock's mom often asked, "What if that was an angel? What if that was God or the Creator?" There was always a spiritual aspect to the discussions Sock and her sister, Cora, had with their mom. But it wasn't just her mom. It was her aunts, her uncle, and her grandparents.

While that spirituality is shared by everyone in the community, some have had encounters with the spirit world of a more unusual kind. Sock was told at a young age that she and her friends Sheri and Julie had had past experiences that would help them to interview witnesses of inexplicable phenomena. The three of them have made it their mission to record the experiences of their people.

"Our people don't have a tradition of recording the history of their paranormal experiences," she admitted. "That's why we stepped up and did the book." The three women co-wrote the book *L'Nu'k Ghost Stories of PEI* to share the encounters of the Mi'kmaq nation.

"My passion is documenting these ghost stories that we hear," she said, adding that their ultimate goal is to get the stories shared through a more visual medium.

There is support from the Mi'kmaq community for the work Sock, Bernard, and Pellissier-Lush do. Both Chief Junior Gould, of Abegweit First Nation, and former Chief Darlene Bernard, of Lennox Island First Nation, have expressed openness to their work. Bernard stepped down in April 2025, setting up an election in June.

Their work takes them across the island province. One location that caught the Mi'kmaq Paranormal team's attention as they were travelling was Beaconsfield Historic House.

Mi'kmaq paranormal investigator Tee Sock and her team investigated the Beaconsfield Historic House in Charlottetown in 2019. The team witnessed the apparition of part of a woman in the windows of the front door.

It is said that the ghost of a woman and her children can be seen glaring out one of the windows.[10] Sock captured a woman's image, but not in the expected third-floor window. On the evening they visited the house, a team member, Gilbert Sark, directed Sock's attention to the front door.

"I didn't catch it at first, so he kept saying, 'Look at the front door. There's a ghost in the window,'" she recalled. "When I actually heard what he said, I looked at the front door. And we started taking pictures. Sure enough, there was a woman who was in 1920s garb: tight shirt with a collar and hair in a bun. She was standing there and then faded off."

The team, which includes the three co-founders and ten active members, has investigated locations beyond Charlottetown, including Yeo House in Tyne Valley, Goblin Hollow, Barlow Road, and West Point Lighthouse.

Located on the westernmost tip of Prince Edward Island, West Point Lighthouse (it's not just a clever name) was first lit on December 21, 1875. It was fully functioning by May 21, 1876. Now an inn, it's suspected — stop me if you've heard this one before — to be haunted by a former lighthouse keeper, William Anderson MacDonald.[11] The lighthouse also has its collection of pirate booty stories, as shared by Julie Watson in her book *Ghost Stories and Legends of Prince Edward Island.*

Sock and her team performed experiments to make contact with MacDonald using a P-SB11 Spirit Box, a tool that uses radio waves to reveal the presence of spirits. It has been known to reveal intelligent hauntings.

"The sound was so good that we were able to rewind it and actually make out the answers," she recalled. "It was just a fascinating place to spend the night walking up and down from the top of the lighthouse to the bottom."

They caught an image of a person's hand in the mirror when they shot photos at the lighthouse and the adjoining building. They're not quite sure if the hand was MacDonald's, but it didn't belong to any of the three ladies.

It's easy to get swept up in ghost stories. They keep us captivated, and there really is a magnetic draw to them.

There is a personal aspect with some of the investigations that Sock and her team undertake. In some cases, they are helping those in need. No promises are made to "clean" a house, but Sock is always willing to perform a smudging or provide dreamcatchers for any children involved in a private residence they are investigating. Those investigations hit home for her.

The need to help comes from understanding what trauma does to a person. Sock has seen that firsthand in her family. Her mother, Mary (Katherine) Knockwood Archer, was a residential school survivor. She attended Shubenacadie Indian Residential School, which operated from 1929 to 1967, during the 1950s.

I spoke to Sock before for a lengthy feature in *Haunted Magazine* about the experience she had with her mother when they visited the shell of the former school. "Seeing the paranormal effect that it had on my mother was fascinating to me. I felt sorry [for my mom], but it was fascinating to me," Sock said, revisiting her trip with her mom.

Sock's mom was an empath — a person who can sense the thoughts, energy, and feelings of those around them. "She was very sensitive to the spirit being around her," Sock recalled. "When we there at the grounds of Shubenacadie, where she actually went to school, you could actually hear kids crying or chatting. There was no adult presence. You could only hear children.

"Mom told me that they were stuck there. She told me that we have to bring them with us in order to set them free from this place," she added. "That always made me feel really terrible about what my mom went through."

Knockwood Archer died in 2018. Sock wonders if her mom's spirit returned to Shubenacadie as a child. "Was she able to guide these children out of that place?"

You hear the sadness in Sock's voice when she shares her experience as a direct descendant of a residential school survivor, and as a survivor herself of the Sixties Scoop. That's why, whenever Mi'kmaq Paranormal works in a case where there are children involved, extra care is taken to address them, to comfort them, and to help them deal with the spirit world.

In the effort to effect Indigenous reconciliation, it helps to have the right elders in place. Sock was quick to laud the work of Chief Gould of her reserve, Abegweit First Nation, as he has been crucial in restoring confidence in Mi'kmaq and restoring the fractured teachings that were lost during Canada's darker points in history. "We're not from a reserve where we hang our heads. We're from Abegweit. We hold our heads high," she said.

Sock went through her youth having her fingers broken for wearing her hair in Indigenous style. But there was no avoiding she was Mi'kmaq because of the colour of her skin and the shape of her eyes. "It was an awful experience to admit you were Mi'kmaq," she said. "And there was abuse because of it."

Other Maritime provinces have taken longer to acknowledge their Indigenous nations. Newfoundland and Labrador is one of them. For decades, the province of Newfoundland denied the existence of Indigenous people there.[12]

Sock's son Cody goes there and drums with the Mi'kmaq as the drum team there has only just been started. Her son is reconnecting with those fragmented teachings, as are her two other children. Sock's next challenge is to battle the cancer that has metastasized to her tongue and right lymph node from her thyroid.

Métis Traditions

Historical interpreter and musician Georges Beaudry is an incredible source for French Métis folklore. He worked as a cameraman for thirty years with the CBC, but he spends his time teaching kids about history and music. Every Louis Riel Day in Manitoba, the schools invite him to interact with the students, to get them to act out portaging like the voyageurs. "These are campfire stories or stories that were told around the kitchen table because I am of the age where I remember a time before the internet, when storytelling was a basis," the seventy-four-year-old said with a laugh.

He's open and jovial, sharing stories about his grandparents being "die in the wild" Québécois, and joking that his grandfather spoke English, "comme une vache espagnole." His grandfather didn't speak English very well. But the stories he shared, the folktales, left a lasting impression on Beaudry.

"My dad would tell stories about his family coming to Canada and how they would survive," he said. "And my grandfather on my mother's side would tell stories of the same thing."

There were tales about the voyageurs, of course. And there were stories about Li Jiyaab or le Diable.

"The stories about Li Jiyaab would scare the shit out of us, really," Beaudry said, with a laugh. "I remember in the cathedral, in St. Boniface. It had this big eye of the Lord coming out of the clouds in the nave there above everybody. It looked down at you, you know? The thing is, if there's a God up there, there's got to be a Devil down there, right?"

Beaudry admitted that you had to listen carefully to appreciate the importance of those stories. It was easy to miss that when you were young, but they stuck. "Once you got a little older, you figured them out. Even the card game Solitaire had a subtext of the battle of good and evil. If you won a game of Solitaire, you beat the devil. But if you lost, 'Oh my God, it was a tragedy.' It was a link to the beliefs of the good and the bad. The winner, the loser and you know these are all linked," he said. "They're all linked to the voyageur tales."

As in the tale of Faust, there are stories in Métis tradition that illustrate the pacts that were signed with the Devil. Beaudry talked about the influence of poet William Henry Drummond and his poems about the hunter, Bruno, who has a run-in with Li Jiyaab. Li Jiyaab gives him trouble for hunting too much and he turns Bruno's dogs into Roogarou (Loup-Garou) — werewolves.

The second poem, "The Devil," is about farmer Louis Desjardins, who is so poor he can't even keep a cat. He ends up making a Faustian agreement with Li Jiyaab, and his farm prospers for forty years.

Beaudry, with a big voice, shared how his grandfather recounted the tale. "He'd describe the Devil, with his tail and his hooves and the smell. You'd listen to this and you couldn't go to bed," Beaudry laughed. "There was something underneath my bed."

In this poem, the farmer manages to beat the Devil. Louis would sit with the Devil, smoking the tobacco known as Tabac Canayen, or Petit Canadien. He'd manage to trick the Devil and then kick him out of his home. The smell of the tobacco burning was even too much for Li Jiyaab and he would never return to collect Louis.

One of the most iconic tales is that of the *chasse-galerie*, or flying canoe. The tale is about voyageurs who long to be enjoying dancing back home in Quebec on New Year's Eve.

In the story, the men express their desire to return home, and poof, the Devil appears to make a pact with them. They can go for the night, but they have to be back at the camp in the morning, and when the job is done, they are to come with him underground. The men are not allowed to sing their songs or say any prayers.

So, they get up in the flying canoe and it flies away back to Montreal. The voyageurs are talented canoeists, and they manage to come close to a church cross. The front pilot grabs the cross and the canoe stops and flips around, dumping everyone out of the canoe. The Devil can't touch them now because they're next to a church.

"It's storytelling at its best when there's a Devil involved," Beaudry said with a laugh.

Shapeshifters figure prominently in Métis stories. Both Nanabush and Roogarou are spirits that trick or change form. We know Roogarou already. In Métis lore, the Roogarou is a Wendigo. "For us, the Wendigo is the werewolf," Beaudry said. "This person that turns into an animal."

In a typical Roogarou story, a group of Indigenous people who are trapping meet some voyageurs who are travelling through the wilderness looking to trade. There are five voyageurs, and one of them, the guide, is Métis. The voyageurs get lost in a storm. The story might have some embellishments, such as the boiling of moccasins. The guide offers to go out and get food, and one of the other men goes with him. The guide returns after two days with meat. By this point, the other three men are starving. They eat voraciously, then they ask, "Where's the other guy?" The guide says he doesn't know. He says he saw him walk over a hill and then disappear. A day goes by, and the other guy does not return. The guide goes back out and comes back with more meat.

"You know where this story's going," Beaudry says, with a knowing chuckle. Cannibalism.

In the Métis stories, when someone has grown so accustomed to eating human flesh, they turn into a Roogarou. They've taken the soul of the person, and they roam.

"In the forts, like Fort Rupert or the English forts on Hudson Bay, people often went crazy. In the winter you would freeze; your body gets hot and you take off your clothes and you just walk out. You walk out and you never come back."

According to Beaudry, those people would usually get eaten by wolves, but there might have been cases of cannibalism too.

"We would listen to these stories the elders told us and they would stick in our brains," Beaudry said with a laugh.

Beaudry admits that with so many different forms of entertainment available today, the craft of storytelling is less and less emphasized. But he still goes to schools to share stories. A lot of his stories are told in French; he'll sing them and he'll wear his vest with all of his instruments hidden in pockets. The grandfather in Beaudry enjoys the moments when he's able to connect with kids. They love the music that is shared so much they latch onto his leg and do not let him go.

"Now, though, you have to be extra careful about what stories you talk about. You can't start talking about people eating people, you know," he said, with a laugh. "Kids are going to go home and tell their parents and I'm going to get a call."

The element of community has changed. It's foreign to him. But they still play music together. And he saves his stories for his grandchildren, who will sit around the campfire at Oroseau Rapids Park, near Senkiw. It's there where he manages two hundred acres with his wife, Florence.

He left me with one last ghost story, plucked right from the history of the Assiniboine people. It's said to be the oldest ghost story in Manitoba.[13]

In the area around Saint François Xavier, the Assiniboine, Cree, and Dakȟóta nations used the area to hunt bison. Naturally, there were disagreements at times. On one occasion, relations had really broken down, so, as an olive branch, the Assiniboine chief offered the Cree chief of Lake Winnipegosis his daughter's hand in marriage. He arrived at their camp on a pure white steed, which he offered to the Assiniboine chief.

The Sioux (Dakota) chief of Devil's Lake was in love with the daughter himself, and when he heard of the impending marriage, he became enraged. The Sioux chief set out with some braves after the daughter. She and the Cree chief fled on their horses.

The Cree chief begged his bride-to-be to flee on the much faster white steed, but she would not leave his side as he rode a grey horse. They were both shot through the hearts by the pursuing party's arrows. The Sioux caught the grey horse, but they were never able to capture the white one. People would still see the white horse, long after it should've died naturally.

A monument was erected along the Trans-Canada Highway, paying homage to the phantom steed. Manitoba paranormal aficionado Chris Rutkowski referred to it as one of the few statues in the world erected in the memory of a ghost.[14]

✦

Every culture, Beaudry adds, has folklore surrounding ghosts, elementals, beasties, and phantoms that caution travelling to certain locations. "The native tribes had gods everywhere; everything had a life. Today, we know for a fact that's true," Beaudry said. "A tree is a living thing and science told us that through their roots, they can talk. I believe it."

The Mother of All Folklore

Sedna goes by many names in the North. She is both the mother of all sea mammals and a source of fear within the Inuit community.

Her story begins with a visit from a handsome stranger. She had been pursued by men, but none have captured her heart. The handsome stranger manages to win her heart and she becomes pregnant by him. He abandons her, and her father, pursuing Sedna, discovers that the stranger left dog footprints in the snow. Sedna has become pregnant by a dog. Her father, ashamed of her, banishes her to an island. There she gives birth to a number of children whom she sets adrift on kamik soles. The children become the ancestors of *Qallunaat* (white people) and the First Nations.

Sedna's father eventually returns for her, but when he is taking her home, they run into a storm. He is concerned that the boat will capsize, so he throws her overboard. Refusing to die, she holds onto the boat. Determined to get rid of her, her father cuts her fingers off. Those fingers become the seals, walruses, and whales of the ocean.

Sedna sinks to the bottom of the sea, where she takes on her role of mother of all sea mammals. In that role, she controls hunters' access to them. Because of this, they fear and respect her. The Iglulik word for Sedna is *Takannaaluk arnaaluk*, which means "the terrible woman down there."

Knud Rasmussen wrote about her importance and her hold over the Inuit in his ethnographic studies of the Inuit during his travels in the early part of the twentieth century.

> From her comes all the most indispensable of human food, the flesh of the sea beasts; from her comes the blubber that warms the cold snow huts and gives light in the lamps when the long arctic night broods over the land. From her come also the skins of the great seal which are likewise indispensable for clothes and boot soles, if the hunters are to be able to move over the frozen sea all seasons of the year. But while Takánakapsaluk ("the bad one") gives mankind all these good things, created out of her own finger-joints, it is she also who sends nearly all the misfortunes which are

> regarded by the dwellers on earth as the worst and direst. In her anger at men's failing to live as they should, she calls up storms that prevent the men from hunting, or she keeps the animals they seek hidden away in a pool she has at the bottom of the sea, or she will steal away the souls of human beings and send sickness among the people. It is not strange therefore, that it is regarded as one of a shaman's greatest feats to visit her where she lives at the bottom of the sea, and so tame and conciliate her that human beings can live once more untroubled on earth.[15]

Kenn Harper, as I mentioned in Chapter 7, has written a great deal about the Inuit culture in his column "In Those Days," for *Nunatsiaq News*. He suggested I dig into Rasmussen's work.

"They told legends that were primarily designed to teach young people in their culture, about life," the seventy-eight-year-old told me. There were so many taboos and rules that the Inuit followed before the arrival of Christianity.

Harper told me that the missionaries tried to replace the traditional lore of the Inuit with stories from the Bible and to replace traditional practices with Western, Christian ones. They might have thought they had eradicated the Inuit shamanistic beliefs, but really, they just drove it underground.

One ritual practice following the arrival of missionaries was *siqqitiq*: the ritual of converting from an Inuit with shamanistic beliefs to Christianity. This involved eating the foods that were considered taboo by shamans, like caribou lung or heart.

The taboos all revolved around food. When a seal was brought into the home — typically a snow hut during the winter — women were not allowed to sew or do other work until the seal had been cut up.

But even before the seal had been cut up, no one could remove rime from a windowpane, no one could shake skins from the sleeping platform, no one could rearrange the willow twigs under the skins. Oil from lamps could not be spilled and work could not be done with stone, wood, or iron. Women could not comb their hair, wash their faces, or dry their footwear.[16]

There were plenty more taboos related to everything from hunting polar bears to caribou to *silaaqsaq* or Earth eggs. These Earth eggs were warmed by the summer sun and a small white caribou would be born from them.

There was disdain for those who converted to Christianity among the traditional Inuit.

Today, they can still be found in some of the more recent books recounting mythologies and oral traditions passed on from generation to generation. One example comes from the foreword of the book *Kappianaqtut*. Rachel A. Qitsualik and Sean A. Tinsley confirmed the oral traditions have survived the Christian influence.

> The superior oral forms have defied expectations, surviving among Inuit into the present era, with proof of the tradition's integrity lying in the fact that story motifs, even terminological delineations, evince astonishing concordance around the circumpolar world. Recent works have, therefore, been able to take a restorative approach, so to speak, in the presentation of Inuit cosmology, by comparing the most respectable colonial accounts with often-unprecedented recordings of elders speaking in the old conventions and archaisms by which the Inuit world once turned.[17]

Harper admitted the story of Sedna has captured his interest over the years, as has the story of Kiviuq, a traveller who battles the supernatural world with his own unique abilities.

Not Enough Attention to Indigenous Stories

I've spoken with John Robert Colombo multiple times about the lack of interest English Canadians display toward Indigenous stories. He rued the fact that we don't show enough interest in the stories of the Indigenous Peoples in Canada.

The eighty-three-year-old poet couldn't quite put a finger on the reason behind the lack of interest in the stories from First Nations but expressed exasperation at the lack of interest in those who first inhabited the mysterious lands of North America.

"What surprises me is that the Canadian public has so little interest in such material and that the Native people pay lip service to it," he wrote in an October email. "I had to publish the first editions of these works at my own expense."

It's unfortunate, as there exists a rich lore with plenty of legends. The oral traditions and beliefs are filled with wonderful stories. The White Horse story that I learned from Georges Beaudry is one. Colombo's Frog Lake Vision story in *Ghost Stories of Canada* is another. They are examples of how ghosts and spirits form a large part of everyday life for Indigenous people in Canada. It's a culture quite at odds with that found in the rest of Canada, which keeps a tight lid on anything that's called paranormal.

12

Beyond the Mainstream European Influence

Canadian publishing, like the rest of the media in the country, tends to favour the mainstream. When you flip through the various books of ghost stories that hit the shelves in bookstores across the country, you'll find that the stories are overwhelmingly mainstream: white, English or French (in Quebec), Christian. You might find a smattering of stories that focus on Canadians outside the mainstream — the story of Ah Heung Chan running through the alley after he gruesomely murdered You Kum in Victoria's Fan Tan Alley, in the heart of the B.C. capital's Chinatown neighbourhood, is a ghost story that still resonates today. But ghost stories such as this almost invariably show those involved in an unflattering light.

What's going on? Mark Leslie believes that mainstream Canadians tend to stick to the ghost stories that are safe to share. Is the dominant culture just hogging the ghost story spotlight? Or is there a deeper pattern of racism?

Comedian Paul Mooney wrote for the likes of Richard Pryor, Redd Foxx, and the Wayans brothers on *In Living Color*. He shared his thoughts on the interest in ghosts rather bluntly to the audience during the taping of *The*

All-Star Comedy Jam in 2010. "There are no ghosts, white folks, and I can prove it. If there were ghosts, slaves would come back and fuck you up. You do know that," he said. "Oh? Only the white ghosts get to come back? You Black ghosts sit down; you don't get to go. That's what's so funny about it."

It's true, a lot of the ghost story canon in the United Kingdom, Canada, and the United States features white people, white history, and white trauma. And those that feature non-whites often portray them as victims; their stories elicit white guilt. Take, for example, the story of Chloe, a plantation owner's concubine at Myrtles Plantation in St. Francisville, Louisiana.

Plantation owner Judge Clark Woodruff used her cruelly. To try to protect herself, she would secretly listen to his conversations in order to try to adopt behaviour that would help her to protect herself. It is said that Woodruff caught Chloe eavesdropping and as punishment cut her ears off. Supposedly, in revenge, Chloe baked a cake with white oleander to poison his children and his wife. As a punishment for her supposed crime, Chloe was violently hanged and her body was allegedly thrown into the Mississippi River. But Chloe was innocent. Woodruff's wife, Sara, and two of his children died in the early 1820s of yellow fever. His other daughter, Mary Octavia, ended up living until 1889. Since then, it's claimed that the ghost of Chloe haunts the estate.

Canada was not immune to the atrocities of slavery. Even though the Slavery Abolition Act of 1833 ended slavery in the British Empire on August 1, 1834, for centuries, Blacks in Canada were enslaved and tortured. From pre-emancipation times to the arrest of Viola Desmond in New Glasgow, Nova Scotia, for simply sitting on the main floor of a movie theatre in 1946, to today, Canada has been mired in racist, colonialist ways. But we don't have many stories like the story of Chloe at the Myrtles Plantation.

Our stories are muted, tied to historical moments like the Klondike Gold Rush, the Seven Years War, the War of 1812, and the building of the railways. We avoid our darker heritage and neglect our hauntings that have grimmer roots. We're too afraid to explore something that could make us, as a nation, look bad.

Not only that, we mostly ignore the diverse perspectives of the many newcomers who have arrived in Canada from all over the world.

According to Statistics Canada, those three waves of population growth in Canada's history were from 1851 to 1861, 1901 to 1911, and 1941 to 1961.[1] In the last twenty years, we've depended on migration to keep our population growing. And that will continue into the mid-twenty-first century.

We're currently experiencing another period of mass immigration, as the Liberal government set targets for 485,000 permanent residents in 2024, 395,000 in 2025, and 380,000 in 2026. While the numbers of immigrants admitted have started to drop, there are still a huge number of people arriving in the country. And new people mean new beliefs and they add to the culture.

While immigration has been a constant, the ethnic background of Canada's newcomers has changed significantly over the years. In colonialist time, New France and British North America admitted only immigrants from their respective home countries. This pattern continued without much change through to the end of the nineteenth century. In the early part of the twentieth century, large numbers of immigrants from other parts of Europe were granted immigrant status. It was only after the Second World War that large numbers of immigrants from Asia, Africa, the Caribbean, and Latin America were admitted to the country.

In the last twenty years, Muslims have been the fastest growing religious group. Statistics Canada reported in 2021 that the community made up 4.9 percent of the population. The number of Hindus and Sikhs have also grown over the years. Hindus now make up 2.3 percent of the population, while Sikhs make up 2.1 percent.[2]

At the same time, the percentage of people who report themselves as Christian has dipped from 77.1 percent in 2001 to 53.3 percent in 2021. The rise in non-religious affiliation is definitely not surprising. The 16.5 percent who claimed to be irreligious in 2001 has jumped in number to 34.6 percent in 2021.

So, the population of Canada has changed considerably over the last half-century. The identities of the people in Canadian ghost stories hasn't changed that much, though. The stories of the different peoples who have come to Canada from all over the world remain mostly absent from the collections of Canadian ghost stories published in this country and from the TV shows that feature the paranormal.

That's not to say that people from different backgrounds don't believe in ghosts. Below is a very brief survey of some of the stories outside Canada's mainstream.

Islam: A Quick Study of the Djinn

Dr. Abu'l-Mundhir Khaleel ibn Ibraaheem Ameen wrote in his book *The Jinn & Human Sickness: Remedies in the Light of the Qur'aan & Sunnah* that the world of the Unseen is taken very seriously by those practising the faith. In translator Nasiruddin Al-Khattab's foreword to the book, he stresses that theme:

> Belief in the world of the Unseen (Al-Ghayb) is an important part of Islamic belief, as affirmed in the texts of the Qur'aan and Sunnah. The effect that unseen forces may have on human lives is an area concerning which there are many myths and superstitions, and there is no shortage of charlatans who will dupe people by offering "remedies" and "protection," at the cost of their wealth and, more seriously, at the cost of their "Aqeedah."[3]

Djinns are not ghosts; they are not the spirits of individuals who have died. But they are spirits — part of the unseen world. Humans are made from Earth. Djinn are made from fire. And angels are made from light. Djinns are not necessarily evil, but they aren't good either. They can take the form of snakes and dogs. The seventy-second chapter, al-Djinn, in the Quran, describes at length the details of the djinn.

They can possess people, and to exorcise them, a series of prayers can be given to cast out the entity. These are called *ruqyah.*

"Ruqyahs are prayers that you make for a person, generally speaking," Dr. Abdalla Idris Ali, the senior religious adviser at ISNA (Islamic Society of North America) Canada, said to me in an interview. "You can make them for more than one thing. One is for sickness. You pray to God in a way that He either eases out the sickness, removes the sickness, and so on. Another has to do with the djinn."

The ruqyah is used to counter the djinn. It's very scary for anyone performing it. He gives an example: "If I hadn't seen it, I wouldn't (have believed it)," Ali said. "A mother came to me with a baby. It was two years of age. Just two years. The mother said that the child had been laughing like something out of a horror movie. When I held it in my arms and it looked at me and began to laugh. My wife thought it was one of the parents laughing. It was very strange."

The child then began to twist his hand with incredible strength.

"This was not a normal djinn," he said. "We finished the prayer, then something strange happened. The child started sweating and sweating in a very strange way."

Then the child slept. When the child woke up, he acted like a normal baby and started crying. Later when they checked on the child, it was playing with toys.

"Sometimes, it's very frightening, even for us," Ali admitted.

An Encounter with the Djinn

One contact who works in academia shared her experience with a djinn. It was shared during a Zoom conversation once she felt comfortable with me. She asked that her name not to be mentioned.

"I might not have believed in the djinn the way I do," she admitted, adding the experience happened just after she converted.

She converted in 1994, a year into her studies. Her experience started shortly after she converted to Islam. She had the feeling that someone or something was grabbing her ankles and trying to pull her down. Her husband woke her because she sounded like she was choking. She added that the one time it happened she saw a purplish-brown, balding male head at her ankles. She could feel this presence, as if something was lying on her. People were calling her name. As well, when she rose for the morning prayer at 4:00 a.m., she heard running footsteps in the house.

"That was very scary," she said.

"I don't believe in ghosts. I just think it's people seeing djinn," she said. "We're given all kinds of tools and techniques to help keep the djinn away. You might have an imam say a specialized roqyah, but there are also things that we can do every single day to help protect us from the djinn."

For example, at nighttime, reciting the last three verses of the Quran is important. After they are said, you must blow in your hands and rub them over your body three times. In the morning, verses from the second chapter of the Quran are recited. Once those are recited, the djinn will leave the house until sunset.

"That's why I'm saying it's something that we live with every day," she said.

The purpose of the morning prayers is to undo the three knots that Satan has placed on the back of your neck. On every knot, he reads and exhales, "The night is long, so stay asleep." But when a person wakes up and remembers Allah, the first knot is undone. When that same person performs ablution, the second knot is undone, and when one prays, the third knot is undone. Then the person can approach the day with energy and a good heart. Otherwise, they will wake up lazy and with a mischievous heart.

Shedim, Dybbuk, and Jewish Folklore

Dr. Ira Robinson is a distinguished professor emeritus from Concordia University. He was a tremendous help when I was writing a lengthy feature on the Prague Golem[4] for *Haunted Magazine*.

The Prague Golem is a tale out of Jewish folklore. It was during sixteenth-century Czechia when the Maharal of Prague, Judah Loew ben Bezalel, and two other men performed a ritual around a rudimentary human shape made from the clay of the Vltava River. They recited words, placed the word *shem* (name) inside the creature's mouth, and breathed life into it.

The golem would be the protector of the Jewish community against the pogroms, also known as riots, inflicted on the Jewish people. However, evidence of the golem existing is purely anecdotal.

So, I reached out to him again to get an understanding of *shedim* and other spirits from traditional Jewish storytelling.

"Our folklore is filled with stories about these spirits," Robinson told me, "but it's not something that's simple and straightforward. Our folklore has absorbed elements from the folklore of other peoples — beliefs of all different kinds, told in different languages, derived from various religions, including elements of the Zoroastrian faith as well as many European and North African oral traditions. As well, Jews from different backgrounds have different stories, and they're rubbing up against each other and telling each other their stories," Robinson said. "Lots of good things can come out of this creative rubbing together.

"There has been evolution over time too. The beliefs of the people continued to change and shift depending on where the communities were. Muslim beliefs rubbed off on Jewish beliefs and vice versa. As Judaism developed historically, it comes into interesting contact with the ideas, beliefs, customs, folk, and ways of numerous other groups. And there is an interplay between these beliefs," Robinson said.

"There is very little that has been left unchanged, very little that you can trace back a long way," Robinson admitted, "So, some stories are mostly accepted, some are accepted by only small numbers of people ... just forget about the idea that there is a Judaic belief about spirits because there isn't."

One of the more interesting spirits in Jewish folklore is the dybbuk, an evil spirit said to be able to enter a human and control their action. They have become popular in horror books and movies. Some in paranormal communities have become interested in them.

Accounts of dybbuk possession appear in Jewish sources from the sixteenth century, and tales of them can be found in Jewish literature right up to the first decades of the twentieth century. Since these sources have usually been inaccessible to the general scholar, this uniquely Jewish variant of spirit possession has been largely the subject of literary rather than scientific investigation.

Throughout history, dybbuk possession has been seen in a negative light. Dybbuks are always evil spirits. In some cultures, possession by spirits has been considered more positively; possession is not stigmatized but socially approved and the adept seeks to establish a symbiotic relationship with a possessing agent. Possession by dybbuk did not undergo this kind of transformation.

Although Jewish holy texts have described possession by demons as long as two millennia ago (as the exorcisms by Jesus demonstrate), cases of demonic possession were never considered to be akin to dybbuk possession. The former is based on a kabbalistic doctrine of transmigration of souls (*gilgul*) and can be found in mystically oriented Sephardic and Ashkenazic texts. The doctrine of transmigration emerged in Jewish mysticism in the twelfth century and rapidly became a core concept.[5]

There was a widespread belief in the Middle Ages that at the moment of death a struggle takes place between the angels and the Devil over the soul of the deceased. This belief paralleled the notion among Jews that the demons seek to gain possession of the corpse while it is yet unburied. The corpse itself was thus an object of fear. The dead had entered the world of the spirits, the soul hovered over its vacated shell, potentially capable of harming those who came near. For this reason, contact with the dead was to be avoided, and the clothing of the deceased was not to be used again.

This fear of the soul and the spirits and the apprehension that the demons might do harm to the deceased was the explanation advanced for the prohibition against leaving a corpse unburied overnight. The sooner the body was out of the way the better for the living and the dead. The process of burial was seen as particularly perilous — it was believed the corpse was closely accompanied by a spirit retinue during the procession to the grave, the cemetery was infested with spirits, the journey home was made hazardous by the possibility that the spirits had not been left behind, and the ghost itself was an unseen member of the company. And when finally the funeral was over and the period of mourning commenced, the danger was not yet entirely obviated, for the spirit of the deceased might still linger for a while about familiar places.[6]

The idea of the body and soul being fought over is also found in many Christian texts. This belief was adopted, too, by the Spiritualism movement that swept the Western world.

"Spiritualism was not by any means a Jewish phenomenon, but there were Jews who latched onto it," Robinson said. "There were lots of people, including Nobel Prize winners, who felt that there was compelling evidence that spirits fought over the souls of the dead. It took several decades before most people concluded that whatever evidence had been presented was not compelling."

Jamaica: Duppy Stories

We can't forget about the rich oral traditions of the Caribbean Islands. According to the 2021 Canadian census, just over fifteen thousand Jamaicans immigrated to Canada between 2016 and 2021. That same census also highlighted that 249,070 Canadians reported Jamaican ancestry. Of that number, 101,965 were first-generation Jamaicans, 104,730 were second generation, and a further 42,380 were third generation. Toronto's diaspora is a major part of its identity.

Zalika Reid-Benta is a Toronto-based novelist known for her homage to Jamaican storytelling in *River Mumma*, as well as in her award-winning debut *Frying Plantain*. *River Mumma* taps into the oral traditions of Jamaica and the Caribbean diaspora. There is a similarity between the title character and the figure of Mama Dlo from the folklore of Trinidad and Tobago. Spirits in Jamaica are called duppies while in Trinidad they're called jumbees.

The Jamaican community forms an integral part of Canada and is rich in lore. And that lore, which Reid-Benta grew up with, manifests itself in the form of River Mumma, the mermaid who inhabits all the rivers of Jamaica in her novel. The fish are River Mumma's children and she can be seen sitting on a rock in the water, or at the riverside, combing her long black hair with a golden comb.

In the novel, someone has taken that comb and has brought it back with them to Toronto. Bedlam ensues, and Alicia, the protagonist, has to track it down with the help of her two co-worker friends, Heaven and Mars. It's a great introduction to folklore, but also a great map to Toronto, and a behind-the-scenes look at the existential crisis afflicting twenty-something university grads these days.

"I heard tales about River Mumma when I was younger from my grandmother," Reid-Benta admitted during a December 2023 Zoom conversation. "I would go to Jamaica as a kid, not very often, but often enough. And there was definitely some storytelling there."

Back then, she didn't go into the history of it very much, but when she dove into the deep end of the river, so to speak, she discovered that River Mumma was an extension of Mami Wata, which is the water spirit of Western African folklore. "It melted in with the European mermaid and became River Mumma," she said. "It's always interesting speaking to people who are from different islands and to hear what they say about something really similar."

In the many tales shared of River Mumma, consistent elements include her guarding a golden table at the bottom of the river and combing her hair with a golden comb.

River Mumma is no Ariel. She can be pleasant and rewarding, especially if you find her missing comb, but she'll punish you by drowning you. She can be benevolent and graceful, but she can also be evil and murderous.

When Reid-Benta asked her grandmother questions about the lore, she would receive varied responses. "Sometimes, depending on my grandmother's mood, she would change between which River Mumma she wanted to tell me about," she said. "There are also things where River Mumma is one person, or it can be like multiple different mermaids. It was really interesting learning about that and then trying to put that into, like, a contemporary setting and putting her in Toronto."

The Rolling Calf, the Three-legged Horse, and Whooping Boy also play roles in the novel. The Rolling Calf is a legless calf with chains on it and red eyes — a truly evil human soul. The Whooping Boy is often seen with the Rolling Calf or riding the Three-legged Horse. The horse, of course, has toxic breath and unlike the calf, is not afraid of moonlight. Ol Higue (Old Hag) does make a subtle reference in the book. Alicia has a vision of the duppy tree and she sees the skin of the Ol Higue.

During a trip to the Bread Loaf Writers' Conference in Middlebury, Vermont, Reid-Benta was able to talk folklore with Jamaican American writers, and she discovered that not all the Rolling Calves are the same. She found herself arguing with one of the other writers about which version of the Rolling Calf was right.

"That's the thing with oral tradition: It changes," she said, chuckling at the argument from her past. "That doesn't mean that one version is true. It means that all versions are true."

Throughout *River Mumma*, the Rolling Calf changes its appearance. Additionally, River Mumma's appearance and mood change throughout the novel. "I really wanted to incorporate the old hag, but it just didn't fit with what I was doing," Reid-Benta admitted.

The Old Hag is an old woman during the day, but at night she peels off her skin and becomes a fireball that steals the breath of babies. Now, she did make an appearance in passing, as Alicia has a vision of a cotton tree and the skin of the Old Hag is hanging from a cotton tree.

In addition to the duppies of the Caribbean diaspora, there is Obeah, which is a religious healing tradition that blends West African traditions with Christian beliefs. "There's Obeah and then there's Myal. Myal is considered to be the light to Obeah. Obeah could be dark magic, but then you would do Myal to reverse Obeah."

In short, Obeah is neutral, as it can be used for good or bad and can be used to control duppies.

During the slavery period in Jamaica, Obeah was used to help provide spiritual armour in uprisings. After Tacky's Revolt, the British, through the Jamaican Assembly, made Obeah illegal in 1760, thus starting demonizing of it.

"I had to contend with my own preconceived notions and I had thought that I had gotten over it, just because I'd done research in the past, because I was a minor in Caribbean studies," she admitted. "I just wanted to decolonize my mind."

Second- and third-generation Jamaicans have a desire to learn about the folklore, Reid-Benta has noticed. "I think that it's possible that learning things in [university] and then going home and talking to your parents or talking to your grandparents about what you are learning. That can start a conversation in different Jamaican Canadian families," Reid-Benta said.

Around the World

One of my wishes when I first set out to write this book was to explore more cultures within Canada. I learn by interviewing, hearing people's stories, and sharing them through their words. I also learn by reading, but I am naturally curious, so I want to ask people firsthand about their cultural beliefs in the world beyond the living.

But not everyone is open, especially with an outsider.

While working on my book, I spent a solid ten minutes being admonished on the phone by someone for asking about their perspective on a haunting in Canada. They implied it wasn't my story to tell and, assuming I was Christian, asked how I would feel if someone called those beliefs superstitious, about my website's name.

Well, I listened like a good journalist, and I then explained that I approach these topics with understanding and through a journalistic and social anthropological lens.

I'm not exactly Christian. I consider myself on the border of agnostic and atheist. I do celebrate Christian holidays with my family, as my wife is Roman Catholic, but outside of that, I'm pretty much a free agent on the organized religion front, and I like it that way. That doesn't mean I'm devoid of spirituality. And it also doesn't mean I'm without curiosity.

There are so many explanations for what happens after we die in this world, and I would love to cover them all. In Japan, the stories of the *Tengu* (harbinger of war), *Oni* (demon), *Yūrei* (spirit), and *Onryō* (vengeful spirit) fascinate me.

South Koreans have plenty of lore to draw from as well. The *Gumiho*, or nine-tailed fox spirit, is one of the most recognizable entities from the region. It's also known as *kitsune* in Japanese and typically takes the form of a beautiful woman in order to seduce men and eat their livers. The *Gumiho* also bleeds into Chinese and Vietnamese folklore.

In China, folklore is shared about the souls of evil people who have paid for their sins in life. However, they are reborn as *Xian* or immortal entities. In Taoist beliefs, there are ten types of ghosts with specialties: weird, drought, trickster, venomous, pestilence, hungry, goblin, servant, and messengers. In Buddhist beliefs, there are nine types of hungry ghosts, divided into three main classes. Now, a hungry ghost is an entity that is focused on one intense emotion.

In India, the *Bhoota* is a spirit that can take various animal forms. In Bengali culture specifically, ghosts make up a large portion of the folklore. Entities like Aili and Boba share similarities to European tales; for example, similar to the kelpies of Irish lore, the Aili lead people to their watery graves, and the Boba, seen suffocating victims in their sleep, is the Bengali version of the Old Hag.

In Pakistan, *Woh Kya Hoga* (What Was That?) is a YouTube reality show that follows investigators Ali Huzaifa and KD Asad as they venture into abandoned locations in search of ghosts. It's on par with the glut of North American YouTubers champing at the bit to explore the usual locations like Eastern State Penitentiary, the Trans-Allegheny Lunatic Asylum, and Waverly Hills Sanatorium.

Filipinos have a diverse set of beliefs depending on their ethnic background. Most people in the paranormal community have heard of the *Manananggal*, a vampiric creature of folklore that preys on pregnant women. It is a winged beastie that can separate its upper body from its legs.

However, Indigenous Filipino beliefs are in line with animism, where all objects have a spiritual essence. The folk religions are called anitism. The Philippines is inhabited by more than 182 ethnolinguistic groups, and that makes up a lot of diverse beliefs in the afterlife.

A majority of Filipinos converted to Christianity in the sixteenth century when European explorers like Ferdinand Magellan, Ruy Lopez de Villalobos, and Fray Herrera started colonizing the region. The ethnic groups who converted include the Ilocano, the Pangasinense, the Kapampangan, the Tagalog, the Bicolano, and the Visayans.

If we move from Asia and into Africa, the vastness of beliefs changes drastically. In Kenya, the *Nyawawa* are unseen ghosts of the Dholuo tribe who haunt those living in the Lake Victoria region. The *Kalengu* are a group of entities that drain the life force out of residents in Nigeria and Cameroon.[7]

As Canada continues to grow through migration, these beliefs will be brought here and hopefully shared and explored.

What ties us together as a species is the fact that we don't know what happens when we die, and we answer these questions through whatever means we have available to us, whether it be folklore, faith, or science.

13

Discussions with Paranormal Investigators

Different cultures are injecting a new *de rigueur* into how we perceive the unknown. Then again, it could very well be the breaking down of self-imposed barriers through organized religion, politics, and even economics.

The corporate world does not acknowledge the unknown. It plays it safe: If there's money to be made by marketing Halloween kitsch, then Halloween will be observed. Otherwise, it's tucked away in the basements and attics of suburban Canada, forgotten until the next thinly veiled celebration of a pagan holiday.

Most of the book has already illustrated what English Canada believes ghosts and the paranormal are, and some of the challenges that believers and the neutral face. But that only scratches the surface. Below are some discussions I've had with paranormal investigators who have been trying to explore the uncanny. They may shed further light on what English Canadians lack when it comes to opening up about the paranormal.

Jaymes White

What better way to usher in winter and celebrate Halloween than with a Victorian-style séance?

Jaymes White is a mentalist based in the nation's capital, Ottawa. He visits Toronto every September to hold a series of public séances at allegedly haunted locations. His séances are consistently sold out and provide a solid shock factor. I should know, as one of those séances gave me an experience that felt like a mule kicked me right in the chest.

"Most séances aren't as crazy as that," White told me.

A man who experienced a truly jarring moment at that séance happened to share his reaction online, which was picked up by the YouTube channel *Nuke's Top 5*. "The Drag Video," as White refers to it, is something he can't explain. It wasn't an isolated incident either. YouTube compilation videos are very limited in how they present the full context of a video clip. White mentioned that the two men in the video kept mentioning they sensed something in the hallway behind them.

"It wasn't just one thing that happened," White recalled. "It was happening for five to ten minutes, and the man was saying, 'Something's behind us.' A few people were saying there was something in the hallway."

The room across the hallway had a mirror in it and other people were witnessing something moving in that mirror. Then the chair a man was sitting in was yanked from beneath him. It was a natural progression from the movements in the hall to the mirror and then finally the chair getting yanked.

White saw true terror in participants' faces during the Lambton House experience, especially on the face of the man who was yanked from his chair. "From their perspective, it was real," he said. "You can't fake those reactions. You have to be in someone's shoes to understand what they're going through. For all you know, that was one hundred percent real, and we just don't understand it."

Other experiences White, his crew, and some participants have had include three chairs moving at the George Brown House, on Beverley Street in Toronto, while people were in the other room. "People might think, 'Okay, it's staged,' but people in the audience still talk about it because they were actually at the show," White admitted. "It's cool to be a part of it sometimes.

"Sometimes. Not all the time, but sometimes."

White prefers the "tame quietness" of most séances. When it comes down to it, even those who are immersed in paranormal entertainment are worried about sharing their most active moments.

During a 2023 séance at the Foy-Smith House, at 92 Isabella Street in Toronto, one of the attendees was a police officer. The man sent White a lengthy email detailing how he believed the spirit of a doctor followed him around. "He told me, 'I didn't really believe it, but now I can't explain this. The ghost was behind me that whole time.' So, he truly believes," White recalled.

During the pandemic, White adapted his show to go online, something akin to the movie *Host*, which played up the Zoom séance theme. There were some unique experiences White had while hosting the séance — one woman performed automatic writing, also known as psychography, allowing an alleged spirit to manipulate a writing implement in her hand. In another instance, a male participant appeared possessed.

White has made use of the method in the Philip Experiment. "If you tell people a fictional ghost story at a house that hasn't reported any hauntings, then they will start experiencing things. It's a cool principle; the collective consciousness can make ghosts," he said.

Using the principles of the Philip Experiment makes life easier for White because it's sometimes difficult to secure good places for his séances. Whenever White's company scouts out new locations for the annual séance, they face some resistance from older managers. "We find the older people don't want to talk about ghost stories," he said. "But if the locations are run by younger people, middle-aged, they're open to it.

"It's almost like the old guard does not want to deal with the paranormal. They're too scared. They don't want to talk about it."

A location may be the most haunted place in the world, but if the management doesn't want to talk about what's happening there, then they won't allow access. One example White pointed to is Toronto's Montgomery's Inn.[1] There are plenty of ghost stories associated with it, but those running it were not interested in hosting a séance. Both of the cities where White works, Ottawa and Toronto, have a rich history. Oftentimes, a religious background plays a factor in whether or not they land a location.

White always begins each session with the same question to the crowd: "How many people here believe in ghosts?"

"I'm not exaggerating when I say sixty or seventy percent are raising their hands, saying 'I believe in the paranormal,'" he recalled. He's been running Jaymes White Entertainment for eight years, and he's found that Canadians are more open-minded than when he first began the séances. He can't place a finger on the reason why. He paused, thinking about it, and then offered paranormal investigation shows like *Ghost Hunters* and *Ghost Adventures.*

"It's almost become a new religion," White posited. "Christianity is still there, but it's not as prominent, and it's ghosts and the paranormal that's been starting to take over."

During the peak of the Covid-19 pandemic, Ipsos took a poll for Blue Ant Media asking Canadians whether they believed in ghosts or not.[2] Almost half of Canadians (46 percent) said yes while an additional 20 percent were unsure.

That's a large number.

"I've found that the people who say they are skeptics are the ones that want to believe," he said. What often makes White chuckle is when people admit to him that they are skeptics but immediately share three unexplainable experiences with him right after.

"I think to myself, 'Why did you say you're a skeptic if you have all these things happening to you?'"

A lot of the people who come to the séances are looking for affirmation. Those who attend the séances are usually his target audience, and 65 to 70 percent come in as believers. But it's that 20 percent on the fence that he enjoys watching or hearing from after the event.

It seems the younger generations are more susceptible to suggestion, or with the increase in secular ideologies, they are simply more open to it.

Does White believe in ghosts?

"I like to stay neutral," he said. "I think that helps my job, makes my job a little easier because I tailor my séances to everyone. I know it's kind of a cop-out answer, but it's one of those things. I want to believe, but I also don't want to believe."

Like everyone, White does find himself wanting to know what's next for us after death. That's what draws White in. He lost his mother, Meena Sones, in 2023, and there's more empathy for those who visit mediums in an attempt to connect to the other side.

"After losing my mom, I would do anything to see her again," he admitted. "So, I can see why mediumship and paranormal are so big, because you want to believe there's something more."

Angel Morgan

Angel Morgan is a psychic, medium, and animal communicator. She travels the country and connects with audiences, digging into their subconscious with the help of her guides. She's been doing audience readings since 2015.

It's the day after one of her performances, and we're discussing why Canadians have hang-ups when it comes to the paranormal and why they avoid talking about the subject altogether.

"White Canadians don't like to talk about ghosts," she said. "Indigenous have no problem talking about the spirit world. That's a really big difference. The Puritan way of thinking, to some small degree, is there. There is this sense of fear of that unknown," she admitted. "It's not even the unknown. It's the dark part of it."

We typically don't talk about the hard stuff, which was obvious by how the whole country reacted when 215 bodies were discovered in unmarked graves on the Kamloops Residential School grounds in May 2021. There were lots of stories in the media, and even though average Canadians were hesitant to talk about the residential school graves, it prompted public reaction, including a greater desire to learn more about the legacy of the institutions.

Also, Canada Day celebrations were muted in 2021 due to not only the Covid-19 pandemic but also the nation's reckoning with the country's past treatment of Indigenous people. National Day for Truth and Reconciliation was first observed as a federal statutory holiday on September 30, 2021.

When Canadians feel deeply passionate about the wrongs that have been committed against them or others, they will unite. History aside, we just need the proper audience to open up to. And perhaps the right time.

As I've highlighted earlier in the book, the interest in the paranormal and all topics related to evidence of an afterlife sit just beneath the surface. An underground river? Yes.

So many people have an interest but are often too afraid to open up about an experience, no matter how banal or easily explained it is. But given the right comfort zone, people will open up.

Mark Leslie Lefebvre opened up about the challenges he faces writing stories in the horror and speculative fiction genres. And perhaps it's because our arts community doesn't explore other mediums for storytelling as much as other countries.

Our arts communities often avoid the stories that we use to explain the afterlife. For example, Hagar Shipley's story from Margaret Laurence's *The Stone Angel* becomes more of an allegorical literary exposition that details her refusal to be placed into a nursing home at the age of 90.

"You look at Mexico and they have *Día de los Muertos*, and the religion is so incredible because I studied them and they believe that when you embrace death, you can enjoy life because now you're free," Angel Morgan said.

Canada honours their fallen soldiers through more sombre observances like Remembrance Day and fallen workers during our National Day of Mourning on April 28. However, in the aftermath of the pandemic, Ottawa began its Day of the Dead celebration in the ByWard Market back in 2016.[3] So, the prevailing trend in Canada is one that is opening up, becoming more responsive to exploring these questions about death, dying, and the ghosts that haunt us.

Conclusion

> To fully understand the existence of ghosts, one needs to come to grips with the nature of life — and death. Ghosts, apparitions, messages from beyond and psychic experiences involving a loved one or friend who has passed away all presuppose that the receiver or observer accepts the reality of another dimension into which we all pass at one time or another.
>
> — HANS HOLZER, *Ghosts: True Encounters with the World Beyond*

I weighed heavily on interviews in this book because the supernatural is best experienced anecdotally. It is essentially a study of people and their beliefs.

While writing this book, I have learned so much about this wonderful country of ours. We do have an interest in ghosts. It's there; it's just hidden behind the facade of Canadiana: politeness, humility, and comfort.

To get people to open up, you need to make them feel comfortable, to show humility and politeness as a sign of respect.

Since starting the book, I interviewed Morgan Knudsen again for a different article, and she said something that resonated. As a researcher, she wants to talk to the people.

And so I did just that for this book.

As I pull together my conclusion from interviewing an array of Canadians, one American, and one Briton, I realize that we really do have an interest in the paranormal. We just don't have the outlet for it. So, we live vicariously through the British and the Americans because we're too afraid to put ourselves out there and offend our fellow Canadians or others.

There's a cultural echo that is more open to the paranormal. What I mean by that is certain generations are more exposed to a cultural phenomenon and it's passed down from one to another through art or pop culture.

We're living in an echo right now. I'm fascinated by what people believe and what our thresholds are for the bizarre.

If we took the generation that loved horror theatre, or phantasmagoria, in the 1860s, and then took that openness and passed it on to youngsters at that time, you'd see them involved in Spiritualism in the 1880s and 1890s. Go forward twenty more years, and you'll get the interest in the 1920s in the paranormal and folklore and people making movies like *Nosferatu*. Then again with the Universal Monsters, and then again with the resurgence of supernatural horror in the 1970s and 1980s. Finally, you have the glut of paranormal TV shows now, and that's thanks to Gen Xers growing up in the time of *The Exorcist* right up until *Lady in White*.

On the academic side, ghosts are a part of the field of parapsychology. Academics might pooh-pooh that field, which includes psychokinesis, clairvoyance, poltergeists, and survival after death, which really is just another name for ghosts. It is a part of our identity as much as the arts, sports, politics, and spirituality.

Our relationship with ghosts as a nation may be frayed because of the glut of paranormal shows, movies, and other media that make the paranormal a circus. It seems that there's that one moment in time where something feels disingenuous and, in turn, encourages a social transformation. In the past, amid the case against Spiritualism, and once the Fox Sisters were exposed as frauds, the phenomenon died down and was scuttled away from the public.

Maybe the moment Gen Xers and millennials had their paranormal renaissance was *Most Haunted* with Yvette Fielding. That was one of the first shows that cast a green glow over night-time investigations.

Then came the running gong show that democratized the study of ghosts and put it into the hands of New England plumbers or Illinois-raised, Michigan-educated, Nevada-residing documentarians who scream "Demon!" whenever the floorboards creak.

During eight weeks in 2024, I took part in a parapsychology course, and the teacher, Elliott Van Dusen, stressed that parapsychology was a social science.

To be honest, what do we measure? EMF detectors measure AC electromagnetic fields, but do we really know if ghosts manipulate magnetic fields?

Whenever I shared with people that I was writing a book about the paranormal, they asked if I was taking a scientific approach. I shrugged. I'm a journalist. I went to university for archaeology, anthropology, and geography, with a dash of English lit. They're all social sciences, save for the artsy English, so I approached this book through a social anthropological lens.

As a journalist with that academic background, I love to explore what people believe through their art, spirituality, and environmental constraints.

Now, as reserved as Canadians can be when it comes to talking about ghosts, it's still one of the most enjoyed ways of learning about our history.

We learn about the social-political climates of the past. We learn about the sorrows and plights of those trying to grow new roots in a new country. We learn about the traumas inflicted on Indigenous Peoples because the British or French were trying to forcibly convert people. We learn about the shipbuilding industry that buoyed the Maritimes. We understand the risks of ocean travel with the ghost ship tales that dot our waterways from Newfoundland to Chaleur Bay, to Lake Laberge in the Yukon, to the tip of Vancouver Island where the SS *Valencia* has been seen.

This is how we come to terms with the ghosts that haunt us. This is how we make peace with our ancestors, by sharing their trials and tribulations and making them present.

If we have learned anything from events like the Philip Experiment, we are more than capable of willing a thought into existence.

Canada Has Plenty of History

Paranormal investigator Michelle Desrochers was one of the first contacts I made within the paranormal community as a journalist.

It was back in October 2013, when I was working for the *Town Crier*, a community newspaper in Toronto, and covering a Halloween event. My editor, Dan Hoddinott, knew my predilection to all things uncanny, so off I was sent to chat with Desrochers and partake in the night's festivities. She was running a public ghost investigation at Casa Loma before Liberty Group took over ownership.

When I told her I was writing a book about ghosts and Canadians' reluctant relationship with them, she was thrilled.

"People have been at me to write a book for a lot of years," the Sudbury-born, Niagara resident admitted during a Zoom conversation. "I don't have that kind of time."

She laughed. But thankfully one of the most recognizable Canadian faces in the paranormal community is willing to give up her time to chat with me.

I thought it only right to close out the book with our conversation about Canada and why we're as quiet as the grave when it comes to ghosts.

"You could do a book on the different cultural studies of all of it. People immigrate here and they bring their belief systems with them," she said. "Halloween is a perfect example of all that originated in Ireland. And it wasn't pumpkins."

True, the Irish carved jack-o-lanterns out of turnips.

Vegetables aside, I wanted to get to the root of what vibe Canadians give off when it comes to the paranormal. Desrochers has been investigating the paranormal for over two decades, and these days she can be found hosting *The Outer Realm Radio* with Amelia Pisano.

I've had the pleasure of being a guest on the show twice, talking about the lack of diversity in the paranormal world, as well as the stigma facing paranormal investigators in Canada.

"I never came into this industry to do what I did to the extent of what I did," she admitted.

Desrochers started doing ghost tours in Burlington because she's been a medium her entire life and worked with other investigators on projects in the past.

"I never did anything much with [mediumship] and I started, okay, I'm going to do the tours," she said. She brought in one hundred people in one night.

When she worked on the tours at Casa Loma in Toronto, she was bringing 125 people a night to the landmark.

"It started as one night a month," she admitted. "And they just kept asking me, can we just keep adding nights? I'm like, sure, because I love doing it."

It seemed bizarre, though, that a traditional organization like Kiwanis, a group of older gentlemen who didn't want to talk about ghosts, wanted to host ghost tours at the home of Sir Henry Pellatt.

"They realized that people were coming through the castle over the course of fifty years and sending letters. The curator at the time showed me handwritten letters that had come in over the years."

The interest has been there for quite a while.

Commercially speaking, there's always been an interest, especially when it comes to pop culture. From the old black-and-white marvels of the Universal Monsters to the Hammer Film productions to the *Ghostbusters* era, our fascination with the uncanny has always captivated our imaginations.

Desrochers admitted that *Most Haunted* brought the investigation-style TV show to the forefront, but ghosts were always popular in the United Kingdom.

"I started learning by doing it, that it started opening doors that would otherwise be off limits," she admitted, adding the Elgin Theatre in Toronto was one such example. She was able to explore that location, with the permission of its reserved manager, for a show called "Living in Toronto."

That was back in 2007. The Elgin Theatre requested her and her colleague at the time, Pat Cross, and they filmed. Typically, they don't allow people on the stage. But in this instance, Desrochers went up on the stage and saw the old Vaudeville backdrops, and the manager then brought her downstairs.

He revealed an old well. There was an old farmhouse under the grand staircase of the Elgin Winter Garden Theatre on Yonge Street.

"Then he started telling me all of these ghost stories," she recalled. "He goes, 'I've been here twenty years and I've seen so much stuff.'"

It all depends on the establishment, and it can turn on a dime. While Desrochers was running the Casa Loma tours, she would be sent to libraries and senior homes and some of the residents of the homes would share ghost stories.

"I think the experiences have always been there," Desrochers said. "I feel that maybe because of the sign of the times, it's a family secret. 'You don't talk about that; the neighbours will think we're crazy.'"

It's just as much about history as it is about the ghosts.

Desrochers is thankful for her time with Casa Loma as she learned so much about the iconic building that sits atop Baldwin Steps. Most of the ghost stories hidden within those walls were never shared as Desrochers and her Casa Loma team wanted to see how many people could pick up the real experiences.

And then there's the alleged third tunnel under the mansion, one that people suspect went to the hunting lodge.

Desrochers has been all over the world, experiencing many different places and different paranormal experiences.

And that's why, for Desrochers, ghost stories matter to a nation's cultural identity.

"Our Indigenous people and Indigenous people all over the world — ancient cultures have left traces through oral history, through petroglyphs, through structures," she said. "Every story deserves to be told."

She admitted the media has ruined anything paranormal because, for Desrochers, it labels you.

"The whole world probably thinks I run around screaming demon, and I'm probably the most logical person ever, going 'No, it's psychokinesis,'" she said, with a laugh. "I'm a real bugger that way. But [the media] labels a lot of different things, so you can't really appreciate things for what they truly are."

"A good ghost story has to be accompanied by good history," she added. "And if it's not, then how do you have an understanding of something that's haunted if you don't understand the history of the location?"

That's the starting point of every investigation. You have to love history and you have to love science. Whenever Desrochers gets the chance to teach children about the inexplicable, she stresses those interests.

"You have to find a logical way to explain what you're seeing. You don't just take it at face value," she said. "Unfortunately, there's too much of that.

"But to truly honour the old tales — the Wendigo, the Sasquatch, and the tales of this place is haunted — you have to understand where it all began."

Not all houses are haunted. Not all cemeteries are haunted.

Additionally, when there is shared trauma around the world, there is an increased interest in the paranormal. The Covid-19 pandemic created this foundation for a resurgence in Spiritualism. Or even different spirituality.

Desrochers gets excited talking about Lilly Dale, in New York, which is referred to as a retreat for mediums to decompress. But with that interest, that surge in finding the smoking gun, there's a counterbalance. Some investigators are going into haunted locations like cowboys, rather than helping those in need.

And that's where the bad taste and trepidation begin. Still, the world seems to be opening up more.

"I think it's loosening up a little bit because people are more open minded," she said. "Some people view the world from their couch. They don't get to sit there and go out and experience the world.

"I think it goes far beyond just the fear factor of it all. It's just the whole movement itself; people are easing up and they're maybe letting go of the old ways."

But maybe Canadians are just logical. Maybe we're just waiting for the evidence to get on board.

A Small Helping of Skepticism

Northern Lakes College professor Matthew Hayes has written about UFOs and the conspiracy culture behind them in his tome *Search for the Unknown: Canada's UFO Files and the Rise of Conspiracy Theory*. But my pressing question for him was whether the belief in ghosts has the same stigma.

Are people who believe in ghosts just as nuanced — read quirky — as those who search the skies for flashing lights?

"In a general way, Canadians are experiencing stuff but just are much more reluctant to talk about it," he said, during an October 2023 Zoom conversation.

It could be part of our cultural fabric as Canadians not to take risks.

"I would say that in very broad strokes a lot of our culture and politics comes from Britain," Hayes said. "Prior to the Second World War, we were servants of the Crown. We basically just went along with everything, and the British are famously very reserved.

"They don't like talking about embarrassing things, especially like paranormal activity they've experienced."

Canadians began to push back against both the United Kingdom and the United States and started to develop our own culture.

"We can't just be Americans," he said. "There's just this push and pull happening from both sides historically and geographically. It becomes this awful mix where you just get Canadians afraid to talk about anything for fear of embarrassment."

That has been a resounding theme throughout our politics. Hayes pointed to our longest-serving prime minister, William Lyon Mackenzie King, serving for 21 years and 154 days.

"He was explicitly elected on these platforms of let's be cautious," he said. "Let's not make any bold statements or bold moves. We're going to wait and see what everybody else is doing."

Ironically, William Lyon Mackenzie King was curious about the nature of the afterlife and was a known spiritualist.[1] One article, written by Percy Philip, was actually an interview with the former prime minister four years after he died. Being Scottish, Philip used that as his explanation in his CBC Radio interview with King in a follow-up piece in *Liberty Magazine*, referring to King as being "fey" or giving the impression of vague unworldliness.

> It was not until after his death that the Canadian people learned that their bachelor, Liberal Prime Minister communed with the dead both directly and, occasionally, through mediums. When it did become known — in a rather sensational way — it shocked many. Yet the Prime Minister made no secret of his beliefs and practices.

But all of that stuff, him talking to his dog through mediums, came out after his death.

"Maybe that's some central contradiction in Canadian culture; it's the difference between front stage and backstage," Hayes admitted. "The culture doesn't really change enough to take [King's spiritualism] seriously until the sixties or even the seventies."

The attitudes toward the inexplicable are changing, with even more scholars willing to talk more, Hayes has observed. Geography professor Paul Kingsbury at Simon Fraser University is one example of this.

There is still a lot of ambiguity behind it all, and the technology used, in the modern parlance of our times, is sus.

"If you're going ghost hunting, it's something that we cannot see, or at least not reliably," Hayes admitted. "There's debate over that. And then you bring in technology, which is also a bit of an outlier because none of this technology is conventional. None of it's in the peer-reviewed literature.

"You just, there's just so much ambiguity, so much controversy built into the very study itself. It makes sense why it's hard to get any kind of academic backing for it."

Hayes's work on looking at the UFO community has opened his eyes to the people who are entrenched in the believer camp. They do not like it when you are not in their camp.

"It's ridiculous how, when the stakes are so low, the fighting's the fiercest," Hayes admitted. "There's nothing to gain fighting about what this really is."

Although the divisive is not as prevalent within the ghost-hunting crowd, there are still a few polarizing figures within the celebrity pockets that seem to appear as the gatekeepers.

The evolution of the culture is palpable though. During the 1970s, as films like *The Exorcist*, *The Omen*, and *The Amityville Horror* brought audiences to the theatres, they also brought demons into the psyche. Add the satanic panic of the 1980s, another element. Now, there are "shadow people," or new folklore created from what scares us.

Somehow Canada has avoided the whole demonic element though. Perhaps it's because we're grounded in a more secular, multi-cultural environment. Or maybe it's because Ed and Lorraine Warren just didn't find us all that interesting.

"To some people, Tarot and astrology and ghost sighting and all this is all the same kind of thing. It's nothing but superstition," Hayes said. "But then even in the literature I've read, there are people who are a little more nuanced than that."

There are some levels of credibility to ghost sightings and near-death experiences that make you question your own beliefs, depending on how they've been studied. But still … Canada.

"Canadians are terrified of being classed as part of the woo crowd," Hayes said, with a laugh. "Absolutely."

This Is the End

I feel like this is the coda of a Gordon Lightfoot song. He's told us the legends, the effect they've had on people and the passage of time.

As former prime minister Justin Trudeau said after Lightfoot died in 2023, "Mr. Lightfoot's music told stories that captured the Canadian spirit."[2] Indeed, Lightfoot certainly captured that humble pie in everyday life.

And that's Canadians when it comes to ghosts. Globally speaking, unlike the U.K., we're not old enough to have ghost stories engrained in us, shared every Christmas through some Dickensian morality tale. And we are aware of this lack of standing.

We're also not as flashy as our American neighbours, who capitalize on anything that has a pulse or, in this case, doesn't.

It has a lot to do with who we are. That's not to say Canadians turn their noses up at a good ghost story. Far from it.

Even in my day-to-day life, whenever somebody learns that I write about the paranormal outside of my day job as a business editor, they will conspiratorially sit down with me and say, "Okay, tell me if you've heard this before … and I'm not crazy, but …"

Acknowledgements

I'd like to take a moment to remember Winnipeg-based psychiatrist Dr. Manuel Matas. I had the opportunity to interview him for the Superstitious Times about his book *The Borders of Normal: A Psychiatrist De-Stigmatizes the Paranormal.*

It was a great interview, and I was hoping to reconnect with Matas for this book because his understanding of the paranormal and his empathy for those experiencing it were refreshing, given the cultural climes in Canada. Unfortunately, he died on October 30, 2022, just a month after I got the green light for this book. If you get a chance, pick up a copy of his book, as it will provide a behind-the-curtain look at psychiatry and how he debunks mental illness as the reason behind some inexplicable experiences.

I'd also like to pay my respects to Terry Boyle. He was one of the big fixtures of history and the paranormal, and he made a memorable impact on many Canadians in the early aughts.

He was the original host of *Creepy Canada*. He died on July 11, 2016. The Burk's Falls resident was sixty-three. Within the paranormal community, he was a fixture, the face you associated with historians, sliding high school lessons in with their ghost stories.

My parents had the opportunity to go on a ghost walk hosted by him in Parry Sound before his departure. Boyle was, for me, synonymous with ghosts in Ontario and even abroad.

He was part of that group of paranormal names that led the first wave of Canadian paranormal books. You know, that group featuring Jo-Anne Christensen, John Robert Colombo, Sheila Hervey, Barbara Smith, and Steve Vernon? Nova Scotian and folklorist Helen Creighton got the ball rolling, but these seven really were the foundation for Canadian Gen Xers and early millennials wanting to dabble in the paranormal.

He was candid and respected the history behind ghost stories, and it was evident in every book he wrote, dating back to 1976. Boyle was a teacher and historian after all. He opened up to us in his books, admitting his childhood fear of the dark but also something else inexplicable. He couldn't quite put a finger on it, but he might have had a paranormal experience when he was a kid.

"We adults may tell our children that their friend is imaginary, but perhaps the child does see a spirit. It may be very real to them. Do we disregard a child's experience because we cannot see it? This is the time of life to clarify those experiences and assist in the development of the gift of spirit connection as something very real and very special."[1]

Boyle would capture a good portion of Ontario's lore within four volumes. He even wrote about Marilyn Monroe's ghost appearing in Chalet No. 15 at the French River Bungalow Camp.

✦

This book is a big dream of mine. When I set out to launch my website, the Superstitious Times, the goal was to write a book about the paranormal in Canada and how Canadians try to publicly avoid talking about the subject, unless it's around a campfire or at a Halloween party.

Without Jason Martin and Kwame Fraser, this wouldn't have happened. Thank you for believing in me.

Fraser had approached me before to write something in the vein of the paranormal, but the pandemic hit and the initial cryptozoology tome was deep-sixed like the surgeon's toy submarine at the bottom of Loch Ness.

Fraser and I go back. We're talking amateur-baseball-in-the-905 way back. We would umpire games and throw out overly passionate coaches who thought house league ball was more important than the World Series.

I'd also like to thank my patient wife, Jennifer, and my inquisitive kids, Emily and Matthew, who have become paranormal fans, much to my wife's chagrin. Thank you to my parents, Ray and Cathy, and my grandparents, Virginia Cober and Marian and Arthur Baker, for enabling my interest in ghostly things when I was growing up in the 1980s and '90s.

I'd like to thank the team at Dundurn for their hard work putting this book together behind the scenes: editors Dominic Farrell, Erin Pinksen, and Janna Green; publicist Eden Boudreau; publisher Meghan Macdonald; and cover artist Karen Alexiou.

Writers Colin Dickey and Elizabeth Kolbert also had a big influence on the format of this book. It might be odd to thank two writers who are not discussed a great deal in the book, but Dickey's *Ghostland* is a beacon of light in the paranormal glut of America, and Kolbert's *The Sixth Extinction* was a big influence on how and why I wanted to write *Eerie Whispers*. I'm very keen on the environment, and Kolbert's hands-on, experiential journalism made me feel like she connected with the subject.

Finally, to those who love the paranormal and shared their valuable insight with me — historians, ghost walk guides, investigators, academics, spiritual leaders, consumers of media, séance holders, mediums, novelists, parapsychologists, folklorists, anthropologists, and journalists — you guys are amazing.

Keep searching the darkness with the lamp called curiosity.

Notes

FOREWORD

1 Chris Styles and Graham Simms, *Impact to Contact: The Shag Harbour Incident* (Arcadia House, 2013).

2 Stan Michalak and Chris Rutkowski, *When They Appeared — Falcon Lake 1967: The Inside Story of a Close Encounter* (August Night Books, 2019).

INTRODUCTION

1 Robert Weinberg, "The Group of Seven Movement Overview and Analysis," TheArtStory.org, February 1, 2021, theartstory.org/movement/group-of-seven/.

2 Brian Baker, "Sioux Lookout Man Who Recorded Strange Howls Surprised People Still Believe in Sasquatch," The Superstitious Times, November 25, 2019, superstitioustimes.com/sioux-lookout-man-who-recorded-strange-howls-surprised-people-still-believe-in-sasquatch/.

3 Manitoba Free Press Co. v. Nagy, 39 S.C.R. 340 (1907).

1: A BEGINNING

1 Lorraine Gadoury and Antonio Lechasseur, "Persons Sentenced to Death in Canada, 1867–1976: An Inventory of Case Files in the Fonds of the

Department of Justice," National Archives of Canada, 1994.

2 Morgan Lowrie, "Ottawa, Hospitals Argue Montreal Brainwashing Lawsuit Should be Dismissed," *CBC News*, February 26, 2025, cbc.ca/news/canada/montreal/montreal-brainwashing-lawsuit-1.7468703.

2: THE PHILIP EXPERIMENT AND SPIRITUALISM

1 Jodi Smith, "The Philip Experiment Is One of the Most Famous Paranormal Experiments Ever Conducted," Ranker, updated March 31, 2022, ranker.com/list/philip-experiment-paranormal-study/jodi-smith.

2 A.R.G. Owen, *Psychic Mysteries of Canada* (Fitzhenry & Whiteside, 1975), 199–200.

3 John Robert Colombo, *Ghost Stories of Ontario* (Hounslow, 1995), 123.

4 Peter H. Aykroyd, with Angela Narth, *A History of Ghosts: The True Story of Séances, Mediums, Ghosts, and Ghostbusters* (Rodale, 2009).

3: BRITISH COLUMBIA

1 Brian Baker, "*UMM* Spotlight on Elise Gatien," *Urban Male Magazine* (Fall 2011): 76–77.

2 Brian Baker, "*UMM* Spotlight on Jennifer Spence," *Urban Male Magazine* (Fall 2012): 30–31.

3 Jo-Anne Christensen, *Ghost Stories of British Columbia* (Hounslow, 1996), 95.

4 Gastown BIA, "Fact or Fiction? The Haunting of Gastown," October 17, 2018, gastown.org/fact-or-fiction-the-haunting-of-gastown.

5 Brian Baker, "Skeptics, Investigators Play Major Role in Calling Out Fraud, Hoaxes," The Superstitious Times, March 27, 2021, superstitioustimes.com/skeptics-investigators-play-major-role-in-policing-paranormal-community/.

6 Brian Baker, "Is Tranquille the Victim of Wild Imaginations?" The Superstitious Times, March 1, 2020, superstitioustimes.com/is-tranquille-the-victim-of-wild-imaginations/.

4: ALBERTA

1 Barbara Smith, *Ghost Stories of Alberta* (Hounslow, 1993), 92.

2 Brian Baker, "We Need More Diversity in Our Paranormal TV," The Superstitious Times, June 17, 2020.

3 Barbara Smith, *Ghost Stories of the Rocky Mountains* (Lone Pine, 1999).
4 Brian Baker, "Canadian Writer Barbara Smith Pens Ghost Book with a National Twist," The Superstitious Times, January 8, 2019, superstitioustimes.com/canadian-writer-barbara-smith-pens-ghost-book-with-a-national-twist/.
5 Cinda Chavich, "Ghosts in the Mine Shaft," *The Globe and Mail*, October 30, 2009, theglobeandmail.com/life/travel/ghosts-in-the-mine-shafts/article1348163/.
6 Sean Amato, "'Where Did They Go?': No Human Remains Found on Charles Camsell Hospital Grounds," *CTV News Edmonton*, October 22, 2021.
7 Brian Baker, "Is the Paranormal Seen as a Liability in Canada? Investigators Share Their Thoughts," The Superstitious Times, March 23, 2023, superstitioustimes.com/is-the-paranormal-seen-as-a-liability-in-canada-investigators-share-their-thoughts/.

5: SASKATCHEWAN

1 David Willberg, "Owner Laments the Loss of the Moosehead Inn After Fire Destroys Beloved Kenosee Lake Business," *SaskToday.ca*, September 14, 2021.
2 Jo-Anne Christensen, *Ghost Stories of Saskatchewan* (Hounslow, 1995), 82.
3 Christensen, *Ghost Stories of Saskatchewan*, 83.
4 David Willberg, "Owner Laments."
5 Barbara Smith, *Great Canadian Ghost Stories: Legendary Tales of Hauntings from Coast to Coast* (Touchwood Editions, 1995), 133.
6 Brian Baker, "Regina's Centennial Market Has More Than Trinkets to Offer Customers," The Superstitious Times, March 11, 2019, superstitioustimes.com/reginas-centennial-market-has-more-than-trinkets-to-offer-customers/.

6: MANITOBA

1 Matthew Komus, *Haunted Manitoba: Ghosts Stories from the Prairies* (Great Plains Publications, 2019).
2 Komus, *Haunted Manitoba*, 46–47.
3 Shawn McCarthy, "Liberal MP Reports Curious Encounter in Winnipeg Hotel," *The Globe and Mail*, September 2, 2000, theglobeandmail.com/news/national/liberal-mp-reports-curious-encounter-in-winnipeg-hotel/article4167108/.
4 Jennifer Bain, "A Night in Fort Garry Hotel's 'Haunted' Room 202 in Winnipeg," *Toronto Star*, April 13, 2017, thestar.com/life/travel/a-night-in-fort

-garry-hotel-s-haunted-room-202-in-winnipeg/article_67d91872-d2d6-5b12-860b-e1fdbb6e642d.html.

5 Aykroyd, with Narth, *A History of Ghosts.*

6 Smith, *Great Canadian Ghost Stories,* 126.

7 Gabrielle Piché, "'The Writing Was on the Wall': Historic (Haunted?) Hamilton House Put on Market as Events Company Gags Unlimited Shutters," *Winnipeg Free Press,* September 10, 2024, winnipegfreepress.com/business/2024/09/10/the-writing-was-on-the-wall.

7: THE NORTH

1 Kenn Harper, *In Those Days: Shamans, Spirits and Faith in the Inuit North* (Inhabit Media, 2019).

2 Harper, *In Those Days.*

3 Brian Baker, "Carcross' Caribou Hotel Has Deep Veins of Klondike History, Ghost Lore," The Superstitious Times, June 4, 2021.

4 Leighann Chalykoff, "Doors of Dawson's Historic Home Open to Another Realm," *Yukon News,* October 4, 2007, yukon-news.com/news/doors-of-dawsons-historic-home-open-to-another-realm-6971767.

5 Joel A. Sutherland, *Haunted Canada 10* (Scholastic, 2020).

6 Jessica Davey-Quantick, "The Ghosts of Rankin Inlet," *Up Here,* (September/October 2019).

7 Neil Christopher, *Kappianaqtut: Strange Creatures and Fantastic Beings from Inuit Myths and Legends* (Inhabit Media, 2011).

8 Colombo, *Ghost Stories of Canada.*

9 Charlotte Morrit-Jacobs, "Rankin Inlet Is One of the Most Haunted Places in Canada? Maybe," *APTN News,* January 30, 2019, aptnnews.ca/national-news/rankin-inlet-is-one-of-the-most-haunted-places-in-canada-maybe/.

10 Davey-Quantick, "The Ghosts of Rankin Inlet."

8: ONTARIO

1 Terry Boyle, *Haunted Ontario Revisited* (Entwood Cottage, 2007).

2 Mark Leslie, *Creepy Capital: Ghost Stories of Ottawa and the National Capital Region* (Dundurn Press, 2016).

3 Leslie, *Creepy Capital,* 158.

4 Adam Bunch, *The Toronto Book of the Dead* (Dundurn Press, 2017).

5 Esther Cox's experiences with a poltergeist in her home in Amherst, Nova

Scotia, in 1878 and 1879 drew attention not only in her hometown and Nova Scotia but also across Canada and even in the United States. What became known as the Amherst Mystery is perhaps the most famous poltergeist event in Canadian history.

9: QUEBEC

1 Anna Dysert, "Resurrecting the History of Body-Snatching at McGill," *Do Re Medica* (blog), March 1, 2017, blogs.library.mcgill.ca/osler-library/history-of-bodysnatching/.

2 Mark Leslie and Shayna Krishnasamy, *Macabre Montreal: Ghostly Tales, Ghastly Events and Gruesome True Stories* (Dundurn, 2018).

3 John Marlowe, *Canadian Mysteries of the Unexplained* (Arcturus Publishing, 2009).

4 Brian Baker, "Quebec Tour Company Takes Guests on a Haunting, Historic Tour of Pontiac County," The Superstitious Times, October 27, 2022, superstitioustimes.com/quebec-tour-company-takes-guests-on-a-haunting-historic-tour-of-pontiac-county/.

5 Chris Lackner, "Ottawa Valley Ghost Hunt: On the Trail of the Dagg-Shawville Poltergeist," *Ottawa Citizen*, November 17, 2014, ottawacitizen.com/news/local-news/ottawa-valley-ghost-hunt-on-the-trail-of-the-dagg-shawville-poltergeist-with-video.

6 Smith, *Great Canadian Ghost Stories*, 91.

10: ATLANTIC CANADA

1 Colombo, *Ghost Stories of Canada*, 21.

2 Barbara Rieti, *Strange Terrain: The Fairy World in Newfoundland* (ISER Books, 1991), 95–96.

3 Brian Baker, "Amherst's Esther Fest Celebrates Its Paranormal Heritage," The Superstitious Times, October 8, 2023, superstitioustimes.com/amhersts-esther-fest-celebrates-its-paranormal-heritage/.

4 Smith, *Great Canadian Ghost Stories*, 42.

5 Steve Vernon, *Halifax Haunts: Exploring the City's Spookiest Spaces* (Nimbus Publishing, 2009), 55–56.

6 Brian Baker, "Ghosts of Double Hanging Still Linger at Jail-Turned-B&B in New Brunswick," The Superstitious Times, April 10, 2024, superstitioustimes.com/ghosts-of-double-hanging-still-linger-at-jail-turned-bb-in-new-brunswick/.

7 Julie V. Watson, *Ghost Stories and Legends of Prince Edward Island*, 2nd ed. (Dundurn Press, 2018), 24–25.

8 Brian Baker, "P.E.I.'s Yeo House Home to a Haunted Toy Dog," The Superstitious Times, October 26, 2020, superstitioustimes.com/p-e-i-s-yeo-house-home-to-a-haunted-toy-dog/.

9 Brian Baker, "Newman Wine Vaults Haunted by Its Secretive Past and a Ghost Named John," The Superstitious Times, July 28, 2020, superstitioustimes.com/newman-wine-vaults-haunted-by-its-secretive-past-and-a-ghost-named-john/.

10 "Skraeling" was the Viking term for the Indigenous Peoples of Newfoundland.

11 Dale Jarvis, *Haunted Ground: Ghost Stories from the Rock* (Flanker Press, 2017).

12 Smith, *Great Canadian Ghost Stories.*

13 Desiree Antsey, "Newfoundland's Bell Island the 'Most Haunted Place in Canada,'" *PNI Atlantic News*, October 27, 2021, saltwire.com/atlantic-canada/lifestyles/newfoundlands-bell-island-the-most-haunted-place-in-canada-100650727/.

14 Dale Jarvis, *Haunted Shores: True Ghost Stories of Newfoundland and Labrador* (Flanker Press, 2004), 73.

11: INDIGENOUS SPIRITUAL KNOWLEDGE

1 Brian Baker, "O Canada What Did You Do?" *Haunted Magazine*, no. 35 (Fall 2021).

2 Government of Canada, "First Nations," last modified January 16, 2024, rcaanc-cirnac.gc.ca/eng/1100100013791/1535470872302.

3 "The Story of Bluefish Caves, the Oldest Archaeological Site in Canada. Walking with Ancients," *The Nature of Things*, narrated by David Suzuki, 2022.

4 Baker, "We Need More Diversity in Our Paranormal TV."

5 Basil Johnston, *The Manitous: The Spiritual World of the Ojibway* (Minnesota Historical Society Press, 2001), xiii.

6 Shawn Leonard, *Spirit Talker: Indigenous Stories and Teachings from a Mi'kmaq Psychic Medium* (Hay House. 2023), 166–67.

7 In May 2021, the First Nation of Tk'emlúps te Secwépemc made the announcement that they had found 215 bodies in unmarked graves on the Kamloops Indian Residential School grounds. With that announcement, white Canadians were forced to address the skeletons in our closet.

8 Patrick Johnston, *Native Children and the Child Welfare System* (James Lorimer and the Canadian Council on Social Development, 1983), 23.
9 Baker, "O Canada What Did You Do?," 83.
10 Desiree Anstey, "Ghostly Encounters? Victorian House in P.E.I. with Tragic History Rumoured to Be Haunted," *PNI Atlantic News*, October 26, 2021. saltwire.com/atlantic-canada/lifestyles/ghostly-encounters-victorian-house-in-pei-with-tragic-history-rumoured-to-be-haunted-100650063/.
11 Nancy Russell, "'Chills Up Your Spine': Are Old Lighthouse Keepers Haunting West Point?" *CBC News*, October 28, 2017, cbc.ca/news/canada/prince-edward-island/pei-west-point-lighthouse-haunted-1.4371389.
12 Trina Roache, "The Long Road to Recognition for the Qalipu Mi'kmaq," *APTN News*, February 1, 2017, aptnnews.ca/national-news/the-long-road-to-recognition-for-the-qalipu-mikmaq/.
13 Komus, *Haunted Manitoba*.
14 Chris Rutkowski, *Unnatural History: True Manitoba Mysteries* (Chameleon, 1993).
15 Knud Rasmussen, *Intellectual Culture of the Iglulik Eskimo* (Gyldendalske Boghandel, 1929).
16 Harper, *In Those Days: Shamans, Spirits, and Faith in the Inuit North.*
17 Neil Christopher, *Kappianaqtut: Strange Creatures and Fantastic Beings from Inuit Myths and Legends.*

12: BEYOND THE MAINSTREAM EUROPEAN INFLUENCE

1 Statistics Canada, "Population Growth: Migratory Increase Overtakes Natural Increase," October 8, 2024. statcan.gc.ca/n1/pub/11-630-x/11-630-x2014001-eng.htm.
2 Statistics Canada, "Chart 2: In 20 Years, the Proportions of the Population Who Reported Being Muslim, Hindu or Sikh Have Doubled," October 26, 2022, statcan.gc.ca/n1/daily-quotidien/221026/cg-b002-eng.htm.
3 Dr. Abu'l-Mundhir Khaleel ibn Ibraaheem Ameen, *The Jinn & Human Sickness: Remedies in the Light of the Qur'aan & Sunnah* (Darussalam, 2005), 11.
4 The tale goes that in the sixteenth century, a renowned rabbi was seeking a way to protect the local Jewish people from pogroms and the whim of an unpredictable ruler. He moulded a superhuman from mud — the Golem. The rabbi would deactivate his creation for the Sabbath, to allow the creature to rest according to the Jewish custom. However, one day he forgot, and the Golem went raging through the ghetto, destroying everything in its path.

5 Yoram Bilu, "The Taming of the Deviants and Beyond: An Analysis of Dybbuk Possession and Exorcism in Judaism," in *Spirit Possession in Judaism: Cases and Contexts from the Middle Ages to the Present*, ed. Matt Goldish (Wayne State University Press, 2003), 41–72.

6 Joshua Trachtenberg, *Jewish Magic and Superstition* (Behrman's Jewish Book House, 1939).

7 David E. Jones, *Evil in Our Midst: A Chilling Glimpse of Our Most Feared and Frightening Demons* (Square One, 2002).

13: DISCUSSIONS WITH PARANORMAL INVESTIGATORS

1 Cynthia Reason, "Unexplained Happenings Continue to Startle Visitors at Montgomery's Inn," *Toronto.com*, October 26, 2013, toronto.com/news/unexplained-happenings-continue-to-startle-visitors-at-montgomery-s-inn/article_96aa1772-f833-5d9e-9867-7111c432d5e7.html.

2 Mitra Thompson, "Ghost Encounters: Nearly Half of Canadians (46 percent) Believe in Supernatural Beings; 13 Percent Have Stayed at Haunted Hotel," Ipsos, news release, June 9, 2021, ipsos.com/en-ca/news-polls/ghost-encounters-nearly-half-canadians-46-believe-supernatural-beings-13-have-stayed-haunted-hotel.

3 Catherine Morrison, "Day of the Dead Is 'About Life,' Says Ottawa Festival Organizer," *Ottawa Citizen*, November 3, 2024, https://ottawacitizen.com/news/local-news/day-of-the-dead-is-about-life-says-ottawa-festival-organizer.

CONCLUSION

1 Colombo, *Ghost Stories of Canada*.

2 Justin Trudeau, "Statement by the Prime Minister on the Death of Gordon Lightfoot," Office of the Prime Minister, May 2, 2023, pm.gc.ca/en/news/statements/2023/05/02/statement-prime-minister-justin-trudeau-death-gordon-lightfoot.

ACKNOWLEDGEMENTS

1 Terry Boyle, *Haunted Ontario: Ghostly Inns, Hotels, and Other Eerie Places*, 2nd ed. (Dundurn, 2013).

Bibliography

Books

Ameen, Dr. Abu'l-Mundhir Khaleel ibn Ibraaheem. *The Jinn and Human Sickness: Remedies in the Light of the Qur'aan and Sunnah*. Darussalam, 2005.

Aykroyd, Peter H., with Angela Narth. *A History of Ghosts: The True Story of Séances, Mediums, Ghosts and Ghostbusters*. Rodale, 2009.

Boyle, Terry. *Haunted Ontario: Ghostly Inns, Hotels, and Other Eerie Places*. 2nd ed. Dundurn Press, 2013.

Boyle, Terry. *Haunted Ontario Revisited*. Entwood Cottage, 2007.

Brailsford, David. *Duppy Stories: Jamaica's Ghosts, Gremlins and Rolling Calves*. LMH Publishing, 2002.

Bunch, Adam. *The Toronto Book of the Dead*. Dundurn Press, 2017.

Christensen, Jo-Anne. *Ghost Stories of British Columbia*. Hounslow, 1996.

Christensen, Jo-Anne. *Ghost Stories of Saskatchewan*. Hounslow, 1995.

Christopher, Neil. *Kappianaqtut: Strange Creatures and Fantastic Beings from Inuit Myths and Legends*. Inhabit Media, 2011.

Cohen, Andrew. *The Unfinished Canadian: The People We Are*. McClelland & Stewart, 2007.

Colombo, John Robert. *Ghost Stories of Canada*. Dundurn Press, 2000.

Colombo, John Robert. *Ghost Stories of Ontario*. Hounslow, 2005.

Colombo, John Robert. *Haunted Toronto*. Hounslow, 1996.

Colombo, John Robert. *True Canadian: Ghost Stories*. Prospero Books, 2003.

Dickey, Colin. *Ghostland: An American History in Haunted Places*. Penguin Books, 2016.

Fielding, Yvette. *Scream Queen*. Penguin Books, 2024.

Firth, John. *The Caribou Hotel: Hauntings, Hospitality, A Hunter, and the Parrot*. Canam Books, 2019.

Gibbs, Ian. *Vancouver's Most Haunted: Supernatural Encounters in B.C.'s Terminal City*. Touchwood Editions, 2021.

Gibbs, Ian. *Victoria's Most Haunted: Ghost Stories from B.C.'s Historic Capital City*. Touchwood Editions, 2017.

Hale, Kathleen. *Slenderman: Online Obsession, Mental Illness, and the Violent Crime of Two Midwestern Girls*. Grove Press, 2022.

Harper, Kenn. *In Those Days: Shamans, Spirits, and Faith in the Inuit North*. Inhabit Media, 2019.

Hervey, Sheila. *Canada Ghost to Ghost*. Stoddart, 1996.

Hind, Andrew, and Maria Da Silva. *Ghosts of Niagara-on-the-Lake*. 2nd ed. Dundurn Press, 2018.

Jarvis, Dale. *Haunted Ground: Ghost Stories from the Rock*. Flanker Press, 2017.

Jarvis, Dale. *Haunted Houses of Newfoundland and Labrador*. Flanker Press, 2004.

Jarvis, Dale. *Haunted Shores: True Ghost Stories of Newfoundland and Labrador*. Flanker Press, 2004.

Johnston, Basil. *The Manitous: The Spiritual World of the Ojibway*. Minnesota Historical Society Press, 2001.

Johnston, Patrick. *Native Children and the Child Welfare System*. James Lorimer and the Canadian Council on Social Development, 1983.

Jones, David E. *Evil in Our Midst: A Chilling Glimpse of Our Most Feared and Frightening Demons*. Square One, 2002.

Komus, Matthew. *Haunted Manitoba: Ghost Stories from the Prairies*. Great Plains Publications, 2019.

Komus, Matthew. *Haunted Winnipeg: Ghost Stories from the Heart of the Continent*. Great Plains Publications, 2014.

Lambert, Richard S. *Exploring the Supernatural: The Weird in Canadian Folklore*. McClelland & Stewart, 1966.

Leonard, Shawn. *Spirit Talker: Indigenous Stories and Teachings from a Mi'kmaq Psychic Medium*. Hay House, 2023.

Leslie, Mark. *Creepy Capital: Ghost Stories of Ottawa and the National Capital Region*. Dundurn Press, 2016.

Leslie, Mark. *Haunted Hamilton: The Ghosts of Dundurn Castle and Other Steeltown Shivers*. Dundurn Press, 2012.

Leslie, Mark, and Shayna Krishnasamy. *Macabre Montreal: Ghostly Tales, Ghastly Events, and Gruesome True Stories*. Dundurn Press, 2018.

Marlowe, John. *Canadian Mysteries of the Unexplained*. Arcturus Publishing, 2009.

Matas, Manuel. *The Borders of Normal: A Psychiatrist De-Stigmatizes the Paranormal*. Friesen Press, 2022.

Michalak, Stan, and Chris Rutkowski. *When They Appeared — Falcon Lake 1967: The Inside Story of a Close Encounter*. August Night Books, 2019.

Parrish, Rhonda, with Rona Anderson. *Eerie Edmonton*. Dundurn Press, 2020.

Owen, A.R.G. *Psychic Mysteries of Canada*. Fitzhenry & Whiteside, 1975.

Owens, Susan. *The Ghost: A Cultural History*. Tate, 2017.

Rasmussen, Knud. *Intellectual Culture of the Iglulik Eskimo*. Gyldendalske Boghandel, 1929.

Reid-Benta, Zalika. *River Mumma*. Penguin Books, 2023.

Rieti, Barbara. *Strange Terrain: The Fairy World in Newfoundland*. ISER Books, 1991.

Rutkowski, Chris. *Unnatural History: True Manitoba Mysteries*. Chameleon, 1993.

Smith, Barbara. *Ghost Stories of Alberta*. Hounslow, 1993.

Smith, Barbara. *Ghost Stories of the Rocky Mountains*. Lone Pine, 1999.

Smith, Barbara. *Great Canadian Ghost Stories: Legendary Tales of Hauntings from Coast to Coast*. Touchwood Editions, 2018.

Smith, Barbara. *Ontario Ghost Stories*. Lone Pine, 1998.

Smitten, Susan, Edrick Thay, Dale Jarvis, and Vernon Oickle. *Canadian Ghost Stories*. Vol. 2. Ghost House Books, 2003.

Sutherland, Joel A. *Haunted Canada 10: More Scary True Stories*. Scholastic, 2020.

Styles, Chris, and Graham Simms. *Impact to Contact: The Shag Harbour Incident*. Arcadia House, 2013.

Trachtenberg, Joshua. *Jewish Magic and Superstition*. Behrman's Jewish Book House, 1939.

Vernon, Steve. *Halifax Haunts: Exploring the City's Spookiest Spaces*. Nimbus Publishing, 2009.

Vernon, Steve. *Haunted Harbours: Ghost Stories from Old Nova Scotia*. Nimbus Publishing, 2006.

Watson, Julie V. *Ghost Stories and Legends of Prince Edward Island*. 2nd ed. Dundurn Press, 2018.

Interviews

Ali, Abdalla Idris. "Abdalla Idris Ali for *Eerie Whispers*." Interview by Brian Baker. February 23, 2024. Audio, 1:27:41.

Auerbach, Loyd. "Loyd Auerbach for *Eerie Whispers*." Interview by Brian Baker. December 1, 2023. Audio, 36:39.

Beaudry, Georges. "Georges Beaudry for *Eerie Whispers*." Interview by Brian Baker. February 1, 2024. Audio, 1:21:52.

Breton, Cantiane. "Cantiane Breton for *Eerie Whispers*." Interview by Brian Baker. February 28, 2024. Audio, 39:55.

Catherwood, Kristin. "Kristin Catherwood for *Eerie Whispers*." Interview by Brian Baker. May 27, 2024. 1:22:18.

Corupe, Paul. "Paul Corupe for *Eerie Whispers*." Interview by Brian Baker. October 14, 2023. Audio, 1:33:21.

Desrochers, Michelle. "Michelle Desrochers for *Eerie Whispers*." Interview by Brian Baker. November 30, 2023. Audio, 39:56.

Firth, John. "John Firth for *Eerie Whispers*." Interview by Brian Baker. January 5, 2024. Audio, 28:36.

Gibbs, Ian. "Ian Gibbs for *Eerie Whispers*." Interview by Brian Baker. April 7, 2024. Audio, 1:00:36.

Goodpipe, Erin. "Erin Goodpipe for *Eerie Whispers*." Interview by Brian Baker. October 25, 2023. Audio, 35:44.

Harper, Kenn. "Kenn Harper for *Eerie Whispers*." Interview by Brian Baker. December 5, 2023. Audio, 35:13.

Hayes, Matthew. "Matthew Hayes for *Eerie Whispers*." Interview by Brian Baker. October 19, 2023. Audio, 39:20.

Hewlett, Jason, and Pete Renn. "Jason Hewlett and Pete Renn for *Eerie Whispers*." Interview by Brian Baker. November 15, 2023. Audio, 1:04:42.

Jarvis, Dale. "Dale Jarvis for *Eerie Whispers.*" Interview by Brian Baker. November 23, 2023. Audio, 39:53.

King, Donovan. "Donovan King for *Eerie Whispers.*" Interview by Brian Baker. November 9, 2023. Audio, 55:17.

Long, Tobin. "Tobin Long for *Eerie Whispers.*" Interview by Brian Baker. December 13, 2023. Audio, 44:59.

McKay, Michelle. "Michelle McKay for *Eerie Whispers.*" Interview by Brian Baker. June 20, 2024. Audio, 1:15:18.

Mitchell-Clarke, Lesley. "Lesley Mitchell-Clarke for *Eerie Whispers.*" Interview by Brian Baker. November 10, 2023. 40:20.

Morgan, Angel. "Angel Morgan for *Eerie Whispers*/Superstitious Times." Interview by Brian Baker. October 14, 2023. Audio, 1:04:16.

Neilly, Rob. "Rob Neilly for *Eerie Whispers.*" Interview by Brian Baker. November 1, 2023. Audio, 1:38:55.

Owens, Susan. "Susan Owens for *Eerie Whispers.*" Interview by Brian Baker. July 3, 2024. Audio, 39:29.

Reid-Benta, Zalika. "Zalika Reid-Benta for *Eerie Whispers.*" Interview by Brian Baker. December 15, 2023. Audio, 35:12.

Robinson, Ira. "Ira Robinson for *Eerie Whispers.*" Interview by Brian Baker. January 3, 2024. Audio, 28:53.

Silke, Andrew. "Andrew Silke for *Eerie Whispers.*" Interview by Brian Baker. December 13, 2023. Audio, 39:56.

Smith, Barbara. "Barbara Smith for *Eerie Whispers.*" Interview by Brian Baker. December 13, 2023. Audio, 43:31.

Sock, Tee. "Tee Sock for *Eerie Whispers.*" Interview by Brian Baker. November 13, 2023. Audio, 48:01.

Van Dusen, Elliott. "Elliott Van Dusen for *Eerie Whispers.*" Interview by Brian Baker. December 3, 2023. Audio, 1:40:49.

White, Jaymes. "Jaymes White for *Eerie Whispers.*" Interview by Brian Baker. November 21, 2023. Audio, 29:06.

Articles

Amato, Sean. "'Where Did They Go?': No Human Remains Found on Charles Camsell Hospital Grounds." *CTV News Edmonton*, October 22, 2021.

Anstey, Desiree. "Ghostly Encounters? Victorian House in P.E.I. with Tragic History Rumoured to be Haunted." *PNI Atlantic News*, October 26, 2021. saltwire.com/atlantic-canada/lifestyles/ghostly-encounters-victorian-house-in-pei-with-tragic-history-rumoured-to-be-haunted-100650063/.

Anstey, Desiree. "Newfoundland's Bell Island the 'Most Haunted Place in Canada.'" *PNI Atlantic News*, October 26, 2021. saltwire.com/atlantic-canada/lifestyles/newfoundlands-bell-island-the-most-haunted-place-in-canada-100650727/.

Bain, Jennifer. "A Night in Fort Garry Hotel's 'Haunted' Room 202 in Winnipeg." *Toronto Star*, April 13, 2017. thestar.com/life/travel/a-night-in-fort-garry-hotel-s-haunted-room-202-in-winnipeg/article_67d91872-d2d6-5b12-860b-e1fdbb6e642d.html.

Baker, Brian. "Amherst's Esther Fest Celebrates Its Paranormal Heritage." The Superstitious Times, October 8, 2023. superstitioustimes.com/amhersts-esther-fest-celebrates-its-paranormal-heritage/.

Baker, Brian. "Canadian Writer Barbara Smith Pens Ghost Book with a National Twist." The Superstitious Times, January 8, 2019. superstitioustimes.com/canadian-writer-barbara-smith-pens-ghost-book-with-a-national-twist/.

Baker, Brian. "Carcross' Caribou Hotel Has Deep Veins of Klondike History, Ghost Lore." The Superstitious Times, June 4, 2021.

Baker, Brian. "Ghosts of Double Hanging Still Linger at Jail-Turned-B&B in New Brunswick." The Superstitious Times, April 10, 2024. superstitioustimes.com/ghosts-of-double-hanging-still-linger-at-jail-turned-bb-in-new-brunswick/.

Baker, Brian. "Is the Paranormal Seen as a Liability in Canada? Investigators Share Their Thoughts." The Superstitious Times, March 23, 2023. superstitioustimes.com/is-the-paranormal-seen-as-a-liability-in-canada-investigators-share-their-thoughts/.

Baker, Brian. "Is Tranquille the Victim of Wild Imaginations?" The Superstitious Times, March 1, 2020. superstitioustimes.com/is-tranquille-the-victim-of-wild-imaginations/.

Baker, Brian. "Newman Wine Vaults Haunted by Its Secretive Past and a Ghost Named John." The Superstitious Times, July 28, 2020. superstitioustimes.com/newman-wine-vaults-haunted-by-its-secretive-past-and-a-ghost-named-john/.

Baker, Brian. "O Canada What Did You Do?" *Haunted Magazine*, Fall 2021.

Baker, Brian. "P.E.I.'s Yeo House Home to a Haunted Toy Dog." The Superstitious Times, October 26, 2020. superstitioustimes.com/p-e-i-s-yeo-house-home-to-a-haunted-toy-dog/.

Baker, Brian. "Quebec Tour Company Takes Guests on a Haunting, Historic Tour of Pontiac County." The Superstitious Times, October 27, 2022. superstitioustimes.com/quebec-tour-company-takes-guests-on-a-haunting-historic-tour-of-pontiac-county/.

Baker, Brian. "Regina's Centennial Market Has More Than Trinkets to Offer Customers." The Superstitious Times, March 11, 2019. superstitioustimes.com/reginas-centennial-market-has-more-than-trinkets-to-offer-customers/.

Baker, Brian. "Sioux Lookout Man Who Recorded Strange Howls Surprised People Still Believe in Sasquatch." The Superstitious Times, November 25, 2019. superstitioustimes.com/sioux-lookout-man-who-recorded-strange-howls-surprised-people-still-believe-in-sasquatch/.

Baker, Brian. "Skeptics, Investigators Play Major Role in Calling Out Fraud, Hoaxes. The Superstitious Times, March 27, 2021. superstitioustimes.com/skeptics-investigators-play-major-role-in-policing-paranormal-community/.

Baker, Brian. "Spotlight on Elise Gatien." *Urban Male Magazine*, Fall 2011.

Baker, Brian. "Spotlight on Jennifer Spence." *Urban Male Magazine*, Fall 2012.

Baker, Brian. "We Need More Diversity in Our Paranormal TV." The Superstitious Times, June 17, 2020.

Banerjee, Sidhartha. "Mohawk Mothers Seek Halt to Excavation amid Former Montreal Hospital Grave Search." *CBC/Radio-Canada*, September 14, 2023. cbc.ca/news/canada/montreal/mohawk-mothers-royal-victoria-seek-halt-to-excavation-1.6967445.

Bilu, Yoram. "The Taming of the Deviants and Beyond: An Analysis of Dybbuk Possession and Exorcism in Judaism." In *Spirit Possession in Judaism: Cases and Contexts from the Middle Ages to the Present*, edited by Matt Goldish. Wayne State University Press, 2003.

Canadian Heritage. "Some Facts on the Canadian Francophonie." Last modified July 10, 2024. canada.ca/en/canadian-heritage/services/official-languages-bilingualism/publications/facts-canadian-francophonie.html.

Chalykoff, Leighann. "Doors of Dawson's Historic Home Open to Another Realm." *Yukon News*, October 4, 2007. yukon-news.com/news/doors-of-dawsons-historic-home-open-to-another-realm-6971767.

Chavich, Cinda. "Ghosts in the Mine Shaft." *The Globe and Mail*, October 30, 2009. theglobeandmail.com/life/travel/ghosts-in-the-mine-shafts/article1348163/.

Chivers, Leslie. "Lessons Learned from Making a Movie: The Lost Town of Fort Kent." LeslieChivers.com. 2014. lesliechiversdotcom.wordpress.com/2014/04/29/the-time-i-made-a-movie-the-lost-town-of-fort-kent/.

Darey, Autumn. "The Ghosts of Grey Nuns: A Haunting History of the Grey Nuns and Their Motherhouse." *The Link*, October 25, 2022. thelinknewspaper.ca/article/the-ghosts-of-grey-nuns.

Davey-Quantick, Jessica. "The Ghosts of Rankin Inlet." *Up Here*, September/October 2019.

Dowd, Annelise. "Resurrecting the History of Body-Snatching at McGill." *Do Re Medica* (blog). March 1, 2017. blogs.library.mcgill.ca/osler-library/history-of-bodysnatching/.

Gastown BIA. "Fact or Fiction? The Haunting of Gastown." October 17, 2018. gastown.org/fact-or-fiction-the-haunting-of-gastown/.

Government of Canada. "First Nations." Last modified January 16, 2024. rcaanc-cirnac.gc.ca/eng/1100100013791/1535470872302.

Lackner, Chris. "Ottawa Valley Ghost Hunt: On the Trail of the Dagg-Shawville Poltergeist." *Ottawa Citizen*, November 17, 2014. ottawacitizen.com/news/local-news/ottawa-valley-ghost-hunt-on-the-trail-of-the-dagg-shawville-poltergeist-with-video.

Maess, Donovan. "'It's Very Sad': Regina's Centennial Market Being Forced to Close." *CTV News Regina*, April 20, 2024. regina.ctvnews.ca/it-s-very-sad-regina-s-centennial-market-being-forced-to-close-1.6855619.

Major, Darren. "Canada Looking to Stabilize Immigration Levels at 500,000 Per Year in 2026." *CBC News*, November 1, 2023. cbc.ca/news/politics/canada-immigration-targets-1.7015304.

McCarthy, Shawn. "Liberal MP Reports Curious Encounter in Winnipeg Hotel." *The Globe and Mail*, September 2, 2000. theglobeandmail.com/news/national/liberal-mp-reports-curious-encounter-in-winnipeg-hotel/article4167108/.

"Mohawk Mothers Want Former Montreal Hospital Site Searched for Unmarked Graves." *The Gazette* (Montreal), May 30, 2023. montrealgazette.com/news/local-news/mohawk-mothers-want-former-montreal-hospital-site-searched-for-unmarked-graves.

Morrison, Catherine. "Day of the Dead Is 'About Life,' Says Ottawa Festival Organizer." *Ottawa Citizen*, November 3, 2024. https://ottawacitizen.com/news/local-news/day-of-the-dead-is-about-life-says-ottawa-festival-organizer.

Morrit-Jacobs, Charlotte. "Rankin Inlet Is One of the Most Haunted Places in Canada? Maybe." *APTN News*, January 30, 2019. aptnnews.ca/national-news/rankin-inlet-is-one-of-the-most-haunted-places-in-canada-maybe/.

Nuwer, Rachel. "The 'Rainbow Bridge' Has Comforted Millions of Pet Parents. Who Wrote It?" *National Geographic*, February 22, 2023. nationalgeographic.com/animals/article/rainbow-bridge-poem-pet-death-mourning-origin-revealed.

Parks Canada. "Bloody Falls National Historic Site of Canada." n.d. pc.gc.ca/apps/dfhd/page_nhs_eng.aspx?id=321&i=64562.

Reason, Cynthia. "Unexplained Happenings Continue to Startle Visitors at Montgomery's Inn." *Toronto.com*, October 26, 2013. toronto.com/news/unexplained-happenings-continue-to-startle-visitors-at-montgomery-s-inn/article_96aa1772-f833-5d9e-9867-7111c432d5e7.html.

Regal, Brian. "Darwin Killed Off the Werewolf." British Society for the History of Science, June 30, 2009. https://www.sciencedaily.com/releases/2009/06/090616080135.htm.

Riga, Andy. "Catholicism Wanes as More Quebecers Report Being Muslim or Having No Religious Affiliation." *The Gazette* (Montreal), October 27, 2022. montrealgazette.com/news/local-news/catholicism-wanes-as-more-quebecers-report-being-muslim-or-having-no-religious-affiliation.

Roache, Trina. "The Long Road to Recognition for the Qalipu Mi'kmaq." *APTN News*, February 1, 2017. aptnnews.ca/national-news/the-long-road-to-recognition-for-the-qalipu-mikmaq/.

Russell, Nancy. "'Chills Up Your Spine': Are Old Lighthouse Keepers Haunting West Point?" *CBC News*, October 28, 2017. cbc.ca/news/canada/prince-edward-island/pei-west-point-lighthouse-haunted-1.4371389.

Smith, Jodi. "The Philip Experiment Is One of the Most Famous Paranormal Experiments Ever Conducted." Ranker, updated March 31, 2022. ranker.com/list/philip-experiment-paranormal-study/jodi-smith.

Thompson, Mitra. "Ghost Encounters: Nearly Half of Canadians (46 Percent) Believe in Supernatural Beings; 13 Percent Have Stayed at Haunted Hotel." Ipsos, news release. June 9, 2021. ipsos.com/en-ca/news-polls/ghost-encounters-nearly-half-canadians-46-believe-supernatural-beings-13-have-stayed-haunted-hotel.

Weinberg, Robert. "The Group of Seven Movement Overview and Analysis." TheArtStory.org. February 1, 2021. theartstory.org/movement/group-of-seven/.

Willberg, David. "Owner Laments the Loss of the Moosehead Inn After Fire Destroys Beloved Kenosee Lake Business." *SaskToday.ca*, September 14, 2021. sasktoday.ca/southeast/local-news/owner-laments-the-loss-of-the-moosehead-inn-after-fire-destroys-beloved-kenosee-lake-business-4332349.

Image Credits

Amat, Chris, 55
Baker, Brian/The Superstitious Times, 6, 40, 129
King, Donovan, 114
Knudsen, Morgan, 52
Ontario Heritage Trust, 96
Renn, Pete, 47
Sock, Tee, 146
Van Dusen, Elliott, 123

Index

About the Author

Photo by Trevor Godinho

Brian Baker is an award-winning journalist based in Toronto who is captivated by pop culture and the paranormal. In the 1980s, he encountered a shadowy apparition that sparked a lifelong fascination with the supernatural. This passion eventually led him to launch the Superstitious Times in April 2018, a news site dedicated to Canada's strange and unexplainable tales.

Before his career in media, Brian studied archaeology at the University of Toronto. He grew up immersed in supernatural lore — par for the course during the 1980s and '90s — a passion he now shares with his family, including his wife, two children, and their ever-watchful cat. His two decades of experience include work with publications like the *Town Crier*, The Canadian Press, Torstar Digital, *The Globe and Mail*, Sun Media, *Urban Male Magazine*, and *Chrome Magazine*. Brian is all about capturing the unique and quirky in his articles. Oh, and he loves puffins.